MW00788450

# CUCKOLDING

## The Revolutionary Guide

## Marisa Rudder

Author of Love & Obey, Real Men Worship Women and Oral Sex
For Women

**© 2020 Marisa Rudder. All rights reserved**

© 2020 Marisa Rudder All rights reserved. No part of this publication may be reproduced, distributed, or transmitted in any form or by any means, including photocopying, recording, or other electronic or mechanical methods, without the prior written permission of the publisher, except in the case of brief quotations embodied in critical reviews and certain other noncommercial uses permitted by copyright law. For permission requests, write to the author below.

Available on Amazon Books.

**Please contact:** Marisa Rudder

**Email:** femaleledrelationshipbook@gmail.com

Printed in the United States of America Publisher's Cataloging-in-Publication data

ISBN: 978-0-9991804-3-3

# Dedication

I would like to dedicate this book to all the strong, brave ladies who have joined or about to join the Love & Obey movement and live a Female Led lifestyle and the supportive gentlemen who recognized the natural superiority of females. It is also my desire that women and men experience the joy, happiness and passion from exploring all aspects of a loving Female Led Relationship (FLR) and understanding all the benefits of loving female authority. If you have not already, please join us on social media.

You can find out more at our website:
www.loveandobey.com

Or follow me on social media:

### FACEBOOK
https://www.facebook.com/femaleledrelationships

### TWITTER
https://twitter.com/loveandobeybook

### YOUTUBE
https://www.youtube.com/channel/UCkX3wmd934WR103 hStbzbiQ

### INSTAGRAM
https://www.instagram.com/femaleledrelationships

Marisa Rudder

# **WARNING**

This book contains adult sexual content. It should not be read by anyone under the age of 18 years. In addition to sexually explicit and descriptive content, this book contains controversial sexual discussions about cuckolding, open marriage, threesomes, hotwifing and polyamorous practices, as well as the Female Led lifestyle. Be advised that once you open the door to female authority and a Female Led lifestyle, there is usually no turning back.

# Introduction

C uckolding is becoming one of the most fascinating sexual activities in relationships, and there is growing interest in it from both men and women. A cuckold is someone who takes pleasure in watching their partner have sex with someone else. Traditionally, it's a man who knows his wife or girlfriend is having sex with another man. There have been many ways in which cuckolding is executed in a relationship, and historically, it was frowned upon since the man would be ridiculed for the assumption that he was unable to perform during sex, leading his partner to seek out another man to satisfy her. Today, however, cuckolding is much more complex, and this is due to women taking the lead and making the decisions in relationships. Cuckolding is much more than just having sex with another person and requires establishing a number of rules in order for everything to go smoothly.

This book is the definitive guide to this type of lifestyle. Many critics believe that cuckolding is a woman's way of cheating on her man and getting him to agree with it. But, as you will see, there are so many more complex issues at play here, and cuckolding can take on many different forms for different couples. It will be very important that if you are here to explore cuckolding, then you must do so with an open mind. It would be beneficial to explore it openly right alongside your partner to ensure there is no mis-understanding.

I was once a critic of cuckolding since I believed engaging with a third person and introducing them into the relationship would surely cause a rift that would have disastrous consequences. Cuckolding also goes against monogamy, which has been the gold standard for relationships. But at 150,000 searches a month on Google in North America alone, it is growing in popularity. After investigating the habits of many couples already involved in this lifestyle, I have come to appreciate the reasons why people are obsessed with it. I also have a much deeper understanding of how cuckolding can transform a relationship. Even researchers agree—according to their research, cuckolding couples who act on their desires feel liberated because they can be honest about their sexual fantasies, which leads to more open communication than couples in 'normal' relationships. Couples feel closer because there is no hiding or sneaking around.

Today, relationships are dramatically different than they were 20 years ago. The divorce rate is still around 50 percent and infidelity, lying and dishonesty play a huge role in the destruction of many relationships. But what if this could all change?

What if we could be open to our partner's desires and make their happiness our main priority? What if couples could feel completely at ease discussing their needs and wants openly without judgment? Could there be less arguments and sneaking around? Could there be more intimacy and sharing, rather than jealousy? I have witnessed couples who have reported a complete turnaround in their relationship when open, honest communication and a willingness to try new things are implemented.

In all industries, change is daunting. What if we never accepted home computers or mobile phones? What if we still needed to chat on the phone instead of texting and there was no social media, just in person social gatherings? How would our lives be different? The same is true for cuckolding. What was once a major taboo is becoming much more mainstream, and as controversial as it is, cuckolding is here to stay. The only question will be—how does it work in your relationship? This book will provide a guide for cuckolding and the rules, which you will need to follow to be successful. I will also cover how to start cuckolding and how to avoid the common pitfalls. This book will also offer the female perspective since generally she is in charge and makes the decision of what is right for her and her man.

Maybe you are a woman who is interested in adding cuckolding to your current sexual activities? How do you reassure your man and execute it successfully? Maybe you are a man who wants your wife or girlfriend to engage in cuckolding. How do you introduce it?

This book is going to shock many because cuckolding remains controversial in which a majority still view monogamy as the gold standard. My hope is that this book will open people's minds that having an "openish relationship" with others is much more than just the sex acts. It is about the issues of trust and honesty that are crucial to maintaining a happy and successful relationship of any type. I will attempt to create a structure for couples to enjoy cuckolding and make it a positive experience—one which can enhance and increase their love, trust and honesty with each other.

Today, more than 50 percent of couples have a cheating spouse and many end in divorce, so the old ways are not working. Blame new lifestyles, a society that wants instant pleasure or a change in values. But something has to change. Cuckolding could be an answer to some of the issues leading to infidelity, and there seems to be less lying, deceit and dishonesty by their lovers and life partners, whether married or in a committed relationship. A relationship that is exciting, loving, honest and filled with trust should be the new standard. For me, trust is the most important, rarest and difficult quality to maintain in a long-term relationship, especially one that involves sex with more than one person. No matter the controversy, cuckolding is here to stay. What this book offers is a guide on how to engage in it while maintaining a strong bond with your Queen. It is my hope that both men and women will gain tremendous insight into this world, which can lead to safe and happy exploration. This should be an adventure that you do together with consent from all parties involved.

Marisa Rudder

# Table of Contents

# CHAPTER **1**

# What Is Cuckolding

C uckolding is a relatively new practice or fetish in which couples are engaging in a sexual relationship with a third person. It's different from threesomes because often one partner is engaging in a sex act with or without the other partner present. But in this case, both partners are in agreement and, of course, there is consent with the third participant. Cuckolding is in the same genre as fetishes. Many think that it comes out of BDSM, but it is a practice all on its own. A woman decides she wants to be with another man while her husband watches. The husband is the cuckold and the other man is the Bull. What's interesting about what happens is that, unlike cheating, the couple are in agreement. There is no lying, sneaking around or ignoring any of the parties involved, and so many people enjoy the openness aspect of it. Couples are reporting a great deal of excitement because often one partner feels that he or she is not sexually satisfying the other enough, so they openly welcome a third.

Psychologist David Ley said in his interview with CNN, "Overall, our research found that for the most part, cuckolding tends to be a positive fantasy and behavior. It doesn't appear to be evidence of disturbance, of an unhealthy relationship, or of disregard for one's partner." Cuckolding can usually go on as a long-term adventure or just a sporadic event.

I have received many letters of objection from mostly men about cuckolding. They object to the fact that a woman should be allowed to engage in this activity and they should be ok with it. However, for centuries, men have tolerated and participated in infidelity where cheating, lying and sneaking around their women were condoned. There are websites like Ashley Madison that are set up for cheating, yet when it comes to cuckolding in which men give their consent and often motivate their women to do it, other men strongly object. As a writer promoting Female Led Relationships, whatever a woman wants goes. Period. If a woman wants to engage in cuckolding, then it will happen in the female led world. However, cuckolding is taking on a movement all on its own. As previously mentioned, this practice has over 150,000 searches on Google a month, and there is no doubt the growth will continue with no end in sight. The traditional definition of cuckolding is a man watches as his wife has sex with another man. There are numerous reasons why couples enjoy this, but one of the driving factors is that today, with women in charge and leading in many relationships, the woman decides that she wants to be satisfied by another man who may be better at sex and more well-endowed. Whether this is deemed to be shocking, controversial or downright wrong by the critics, more couples are engaging in cuckolding than you might think, and they are from all walks of life.

In the media, cuckolding has become mainstream. In the Emmy nominated show *Succession* on Netflix, Shiv Roy has her husband sign a contract in which it is understood that she will be having sex with other men. Today, more millennials have admitted to engaging in cuckolding on a regular basis with no issues in the main relationship, and there are dozens of sites dedicated to it. Cuckolding was often used by wealthy couples in which the man was much older than the woman and got to the age when he was unable to perform. In these types of relationships, men often participate in finding their wife's Bull and will watch their sex act. In my last three books *Love and Obey, Real Men Worship Women* and *Oral Sex For Women,* I focus on the Female Led Relationship where cuckolding is the decision of the woman. She makes the ultimate rule of whether she wants to engage in cuckolding and the man agrees. Even traditionally, cuckolding was initiated by the woman, so I feel that it is mainly a female dominated realm. This book will focus on cuckolding from the female perspective. However, if you are a man who wants to introduce it to your Queen, this will also help her to get excited since it is a female driven activity with supportive participation.

In Female Led Relationships, the man's responsibility— under his submission to the female's absolute authority over him—is to allow her freedom, so she can achieve happiness and as much pleasure as possible in her life. Cuckolding, in my opinion, should be approached in a similar manner to the Love and Obey philosophy where the woman is the Queen and her man is the supportive gentleman who is making all of her fantasies, including cuckolding, come true. Why is this so important? Because a woman's happiness in a relationship is mandatory. No man can ever exist in a happy relationship without his Goddess also being happy. I have had my share of critics' attempt to argue that my writings are solely for female's control over men, however, the saying "Happy Wife, Happy Life" is true for this very reason.

Whether you are in a Female Led Relationship or not when the Queen is unhappy, it makes for a very rocky and unsuccessful relationship. Cuckolding as a female led activity is the modern style of cuckolding as the Queen exercises control over her own body, her autonomy from patriarchal and primary male possession, misogynist control, slut-shaming and criticism, as well as her absolute right to act freely on her emotional and sexual desires as a strong, independent and powerful woman.

Let's face it. Women are leading in so many ways and exercising their authority more than ever. In 80 percent of the couples I have interviewed, the men agree that they will follow the lead of their women even though it was not formally established that they are in a Female Led Relationship. So, in general, many men welcome the idea of spicing up their relationship with the introduction of a Bull, and they can still participate by watching or being included, depending on the direction of their woman. For some men, they are turned on by the fantasy of seeing their wife or girlfriend with a man who is more well-endowed or of a different race. In this case, he has to convince his Queen to engage in this type of activity and it is so much simpler if the woman feels she is in control of the situation. Sometimes cuckolding is used as a form of humiliation—for being the pathetic slave who cannot satisfy his Goddess and must sit quietly why another man satisfies her. So, there are many variations and ways cuckolding can be executed with absolute consent from all three parties.

# CHAPTER 2

# History of Cuckolding

The history of cuckolding dates back to medieval times, so it is not new. It recently experienced a resurgence when President Trump came into power when some groups used the term to describe liberal men. They were being called "cucks." Since then, cuckolding has been seen in thousands of articles, shows and movies. The term cuckolding comes from the cuckoo bird who has a habit of laying its eggs in other bird's nests. At the appropriate moment, the cuckoo flies down to the host's nest, pushes one egg out of the nest, lays an egg and flies off. The female cuckoo is very aggressive, and this behavior is driven by the female with the theme of "survival." So, it's no surprise that cuckolding is already a female led activity, although men have also enjoyed introducing the idea to their partners.

Cuckolding appears in literature as early as the 13th century. In *The Merchant's Tale* by Geoffrey Chaucer, January, a rich old bachelor, decides it's finally time to get married, and settles on an eighteen-year-old girl named May as his ideal wife. Chaucer gives the details of the wedding night, the physical discrepancy between wrinkled, old January lusting after beautiful, young May. January's cuckolding arrives in the form of a younger man, Damian. Soon the old man goes blind, which makes him even more jealous. May finally concocts an elaborate scheme to meet her would-be lover in the garden, with her husband waiting oblivious and blind nearby.

During the Renaissance, from the 16th to the 18th centuries, Europe had a cultural obsession with cuckoldry. Women were believed to be more lustful than men, largely because they were subject to the whims of their womb, which was believed to move independently around a woman's body, causing her to lose control. Thus, if a man were married, his wife was obviously cheating on him. This infidelity would cause the husband to grow invisible horns, the ultimate symbol of cuckoldry, and the comic figure of the horned cuckold made its way into fictional songs, engravings, and theatre. In Shakespeare's *Much Ado About Nothing*, a play all about love, marriage, and deception, Benedick jokes about never getting married because it means instant cuckolding. In medieval times, one of the reasons for cuckolding was the passing down of property to heirs. So, women were to get pregnant and have children to continue the lineage or kingdom. It was not uncommon that in the event a man could not perform his duties because of age or illness, women might have to engage with an outside lover. Again, the theme of "survival." Cuckolding has existed in wealthy circles for decades. When a much older man marries a younger woman and is unable to perform, it is understandable that she will take a younger lover from time to time.

Psychology regards cuckold fetishism as a variant of masochism the cuckold deriving pleasure from being humiliated. In Freudian analysis, cuckold fetishism is the eroticization of the fears of infidelity and of failure in the man's competition for procreation and the affection of females. In his book *Masochism and the Self,* psychologist Roy Baumeister did a Self Theory analysis that cuckolding or specifically, all masochism was a form of escaping from self-awareness, at times when self-awareness becomes burdensome, such as with perceived inadequacy. According to this theory, the physical or mental pain from masochism brings attention away from the self, which would be desirable in times of "guilt, anxiety, or insecurity," or at other times when self-awareness is unpleasant.

Today, cuckolding is seen in many shows like *House of Cards* where Robin Wright's character Kate as first lady openly cuckolds with a younger man with the consent of her husband, Frank. Additionally, the show *Succession* on Netflix, the character Shiv Roy has her husband sign a contract that includes a clause in which he accepts she will be sleeping with other men. In a recent interview with CNN, clinical psychologists David Ley, PhD and Justin Lehmiller, PhD, along with sex advice columnist Dan Savage, shared the findings of a national survey they conducted.

In preparation for Lehmiller's book, he surveyed thousands of Americans and found that 58 percent of men and about a third of women had fantasies about cuckolding. To be clear, this means they fantasize about their partner having sex with someone else, either while they watch or while they're somewhere else. Lehmiller stated that "Men are more likely to fantasize about cuckolding, and they do it more often—but there are a number of women who have these fantasies as well, which points to the need for more research-focused on women's cuckolding desires. These survey results show that unlike before, cuckold fantasies can be about sexual liberation and empowerment, which mirrors my own feedback from thousands of couples worldwide.

# CHAPTER 3

# Why Do Couples Like Cuckolding?

L et's face it, most relationships are difficult, and there are so many cases recently in which couples are looking for ways to spice up the relationship. We all like variety. As women we love wearing different outfits, shoes and bags. Men love driving different cars and going to various bars. Some people love being around people of different nationalities, or trying different foods—people want variety, and I believe that they need it in their relationships. As the leader of the female led movement where women are taking control of the relationship, which was something originally frowned upon, I have noticed how receptive people are to this change in power. Men are requesting it, and women are loving it. Many couples are changing the dynamic in relationships because they are looking for variety and many are looking to fulfill an inner need. There are very few relationships that break up over cuckolding. But 50 percent of traditional marriages still end in divorce. It's a fact that fewer couples in Female Led Relationships divorce. That suggests that even though this is a radical movement, there could be something about it that actually bonds couples.

Research shows that four to five percent of heterosexual couples have agreed to have an open relationship. In other words, they've given their consent to **not** be monogamous. The National Opinion Research Center's General Social Survey revealed that more than 20 percent of married men and nearly 15 percent of married women admit to infidelity, a number that's risen almost 40 percent for women in the past 20 years. In addition, some studies have found that between 30 and 60 percent of married individuals in the United States will engage in adultery at some point in their marriage. So, while only 4 to 5 percent of men and women are choosing to be open about their extramarital relations, somewhere between 15 and 60 percent are opting for a less consensual form of infidelity. Cuckolding is not infidelity, and in general, it is done together with consent.

## Why Men or Women Want Cuckolding

Research and psychologists have found that when a man or woman sees their partner with someone else, it can excite them and give them feelings of being proud to be with someone who is desired by others. Men and women with attractive partners get this feeling when people are paying lots of attention to their husbands, wives, girlfriends or boyfriends. Sometimes we all feel good when others want what we have. It's a basic human emotion.

As an extension, sometimes realizing that you are unable to sexually fulfill your partner—and you would be fine with someone else doing it—is also exciting and builds a feeling of trust and control because it is actually condoned by the partner getting cucked. Couples often race home to tell their stories and share the experience openly. Some individuals like the humiliation and feeling of subservience. This is true in some Female Led Relationships in which men will be happy when their Goddess, who they serve, is allowed to choose any man she wants. They get turned on by the humiliation they feel when a stronger and more virile man is satisfying his Queen sexually. Humiliation seems to play a leading role in cuckolding. For some, humiliation ramps up the erotic intensity. Most men who are turned on enjoy watching their partner with someone else, or even love it when their woman laughs or belittles the Bull she's with. Pleasure also comes from this being the ultimate show of respect to allow your woman to do what she wants.

I will be mostly focusing on cuckolding in a Female Led Relationship where men condone and even want their woman involved and have sex with another man. Of course, other reasons for couples wanting cuckolding is to gain excitement from the forbidden. I grew up a very devout Catholic. So much so that I was afraid to steal a pack of gum, much less engage in sex with another man while my partner watched. In my early relationships, I could recall flying into a rage if my boyfriend's eye moved to look at another woman. I feel that this jealousy and rigid behavior caused me to become very angry and always constantly worried about cheating. One of my first relationships suggested an open relationship, and I can recall being so upset about it that I secretly knew the relationship was done. Once I broke out of these restraints based on religious conditioning, I was free to enjoy relationships. I became less judgmental and more experimental, and I have never regretted one day of delving into this world. It changed my life, my relationship and my outlook.

Relationships are one of the biggest influences in our lives, which can be a curse each and every day, or a new opportunity to explore and gain more enjoyment and happiness. Once you push those boundaries, you are set free. So, while cuckolding is new, it's growing. I never thought Ashley Madison would become such a large organization spread across hundreds of countries. I realized that there were millions of people searching for new types of relationships. As much as I criticized infidelity, I was open to understanding the trends and changes happening in relationships.

Our sexual openness depends on a variety of factors including security, commitment, fear, jealousy, possessiveness, sense of entitlement, and more, all which factor into the algorithm that renders our comfort level with sexual openness. Some people are comfortable at orgies, and others are only comfortable having sex on camera to make a video that they themselves will later watch. It just so happens that cuckolding is the way couples can begin to explore these different types of openness with sex.

## What's the Advantage to the Woman?

Right from the start, a woman who engages in cuckolding with her partner fully supporting it has the best of both worlds. She is receiving sexual pleasure, which she may not have had previously, and she has her husband or boyfriend serving her like a Queen. So, the woman is really in the power position. There are those who will criticize, but how a couple chooses to build excitement in their lives is completely up to them. Many report a closer bond with their partners because unlike cheating, they are open and upfront about everything that happens. With both partners in agreement, the couple can control how far they will take their activities. A satisfied woman is a lot easier to deal with than one who is unsatisfied. There are many reasons why women are left unsatisfied. Take the problem of an abnormally small penis and a larger vagina. It would be impossible for a woman to be satisfied if her partner is unable to please her. Should the relationship break up over this one issue? Or would it be practical to try to solve it in a different way? Sometimes men are impotent and unable to satisfy a woman. I know many who have had to endure this, only to end in disaster. For years if a woman failed to have sex with her man, it was justified by many for him to find a woman outside as a mistress. Many men today would still take this route, but if a woman does it and gains approval, it is condemned. This double standard is fading as more women are demanding what they want and need, and a few even have turned to cuckolding. There is not as much research about women who do cuckolding, but the women who do it successfully say that it has made them more assertive and freer. They feel more connected to their sexuality, and overall, it improved their desire to have sex more with their man.

## What's the Advantage to the Man?

The cuck is generally the man who wants to be cuckolded. Sometimes it's the fulfillment of a fantasy. Other times, it's more than that. The cuck sometimes wants to show so much devotion that he will engage in oral sex with his Queen after she has been with a Bull. The cuck will generally derive sexual satisfaction from knowing that he is in service to his woman and she is still his Queen. The man still feels like he's in control because he wants to see his Queen with a man who is more well-endowed or different. Sometimes men have the deep-seated desire to be so submissive that he would allow her to be with another man while he watches. Other times it's about voyeurism, and he derives pleasure from watching the sex act. No matter the reason, many men have admitted to being turned on watching his wife or girlfriend with another man or partaking in the activity. In the book *Tell Me What You Want: The Science of Sexual Desire and How It Can Help Improve Your Sex Life*, author Justin Lehmiller surveyed thousands of Americans and discovered that 58 percent of men and around a 30 percent of women had thought about cuckolding. Men are more likely to fantasize about cuckolding, and they do it more often.

Cuckolding often begins in a marriage when the husband usually has a small penis and derives sexual pleasure from watching his wife have intercourse with another man who has a larger penis, which is one reason many heterosexual cuckolding fantasies involve white women and black men. In a cuckolding lifestyle that is one expression of an open sexual relationship, the couple forms an agreement in their marriage allowing the act of cuckolding, which can vary in degree from just role play for some to a lifestyle of actual cuckolding. In real cuckolding lifestyles, the wife will engage in sex with other men in front of her husband. Properly speaking, this knowledge and acceptance of the wife's sexual activities with other men makes the husband a man who is aware of his wife's infidelity and reconciled to it, usually because he feels inadequate and unable to satisfy her sexual needs, but he still loves her and wants to be with her.

Cuckolding can be a form of mental humiliation, which can absolutely be a part of the couple's masochistic fantasies. The idea of giving up control and having someone else take the reins (or in the case of cuckoldry, having "no say" in what your partner does) can be a stress reliever and a rush of endorphins that many people find to be incredibly stimulating and relaxing at the same time.

## Cuckolding and the Effects on the Brain

When two people meet for the first time, they can develop passionate love, which is a short-term, fiery, obsessive kind of feeling. In cuckolding, this can also happen because of the newness of it. Biologist Alfred Kinsey found the effects of passionate love on the brain and stated, "A person who is love-smitten will often make choices that will seem illogical to others, such as prioritizing the object of their affection above work, friends and family, no matter what the trade-offs. Citing studies that used Functional magnetic resonance imaging (fMRI) technology to reveal which parts of the brain are activated when people fall in passionate love, researchers concluded, "In many ways, the brain scan studies show that the maddening feelings of love are essentially a major mental-health crisis. The chemical storm of brain changes it causes are strikingly similar to drug addiction and obsessive-compulsive disorder. Love really does make us "crazy." So, couples can feel this euphoria in cuckolding that led to the excitement and adventure experienced. Research shows that passionate love can be an addiction and studies found "individuals in the early stage of intense romantic love show many symptoms of substance and non-substance or behavioral addictions, including euphoria, craving, tolerance, emotional and physical dependence, withdrawal and relapse." This could explain why couples engaging in cuckolding seem to love doing it for extended periods despite how controversial it can be.

# CHAPTER 4

# Is Hotwifing the Same as Cuckolding?

C uckolding and hotwifing are similar ways of expressing your sexuality as a couple while allowing your wife to have a good time. The main difference between cuckolding and hotwifing is the "view of the act" and "mental definitions." For example, a cuckold is usually a man who enjoys being humiliated for being inadequate. He has a smaller penis and is unable to satisfy his woman. He may simply enjoy seeing another man with his woman.

In cuckolding, sometimes the dominant woman insists that she wants to have sex with a Bull so it's much more of a female led activity. Hotwifing is much more male led because the husband derives pleasure from his wife being enjoyed by other men. He may even be adequate and get involved in the sex act with the other man. A hotwifing husband considers it a compliment to himself that other men desire his wife. He takes pride in having such a hot wife who is sexually charged.

Cuckolding and hotwifing experiences are similar—a married woman engages in sexual relationships with other men with her man's consent. Often, these relationships are in pursuit of fulfilling the husband's or the couple's fantasies, and this can apply to any woman whose husband feels she is hot enough to attract another man or for the cuckold in which he is not sexually capable of satisfying her alone. In the world of kinky sex, either form of expression simply means the husband desires some level of interaction between his wife and another man.

While the concept of another man holding, kissing and making love to your wife is typically considered to be a bit abnormal, it is a fantasy that many men and women do have. In fact, research has shown that a majority of men fantasize about watching their wife engage in some degree of sexual activity with another man. Today, many couples consider cuckolding or hotwifing to simply be fun, exciting and beneficial to their marriage. It is obvious why women like it since it allows them to fulfill their wildest sexual fantasies. In addition, many couples share this sexual fantasy of taking their relationship to a kinkier level.

Research shows that couples have fantasies about cuckolding and hotwifing but many are afraid to express themselves because they fear what their partner might think of them. So, one of the benefits of acting on a cuckolding or hotwifing fantasy is the real-life fulfillment of your most secret desire. It also provides women with a new found modern freedom and the right for her to choose what she does with her body. Modern women do not want to be controlled by a man. In female led marriage, women have the right to do as they see fit. The wife gets the freedom to enjoy the company of the opposite sex. Many women in female led marriages enjoy the company of men other than their husbands. They practice the idea that modern women are "not the property of their husbands." This modern way is allowing women to have the chance to enjoy life more. When a man allows his woman to be in the company of other men, she enjoys a fresh kind of intimacy and freedom with all her men, including her husband.

In female led marriage, women are freed from the jealousy of their husband. Jealousy is one of the major reasons many relationships fail. Jealousy arises from male ego concerns and their male insecurities. This male ego-based jealousy is a contributing factor in many disagreements and breakups. As we learned, jealousy comes from ancient genetic coding in men to protect their future lineage by making sure that his wife's offspring are his as well. Hotwifing is a modern experience involving birth control, which can help to rid the man of his feelings of jealousy. In a female led marriage, the wife can enjoy her freedom to be who she wants to be. She knows her husband will be obedient, and he will have her best interests and her pleasure at heart, which helps her trust him more and enjoy the marriage.

Relationships are built on trust and communication. Hotwifing and cuckolding increase trust and communication within relationships. If you want to be really happy, with a lasting relationship, you must ensure that you understand each other and also give each other the chance and freedom to be who you really are, including living out your most secret fantasies. Before you begin to dive into actual hotwifing or cuckolding, you both need to agree with each other of your intent to participate. The women in Female Led Relationships are typically sexually dominant while the man takes on a more submissive role, only becoming involved with her sexually or with her lover when the wife permits him to. Sometimes the man will remain in chastity and completely celibate for the entire marriage.

As a man, you may feel that you actually have the hottest woman on earth, and it's every man's desire to have a woman who is another man's dream. Hotwifing gives a man the perfect chance to allow other men to appreciate how beautiful and desirable his woman is, which typically serves to increase both his love and respect for her. It boosts both the man and the woman's confidence. In female led marriages and both cuckolding and hotwifing experiences, women have a chance to express themselves. When a woman knows that she has the support of her man to do whatever she desires, she feels great about herself, which helps to boost her own self-confidence. This kind of open and honest relationship increases trust and communication between the couple and brings them closer together.

It is well known that Female Led Relationships increase intimacy. Cuckolding and hotwifing give a couple the perfect chance to gain important knowledge about themselves and each other that can help increase their level of closeness and connection. The new sexual adventures and the wide variety of options dramatically deepens a couple's bond. It provides a greater sense of sexual satisfaction for both husband and wife. Cuckolding and hotwifing create a lifestyle for attaining physical satisfaction. The woman is able to spend quality time with men who interest her, which quenches her thirst that in more traditional marriages would typically lead to affairs and betrayals that destroy trust and relationships. One of the main benefits of Female Led Relationships is that the couple stay together because they are far more open, honest, intimate, loving and fulfilling than many people think.

# CHAPTER 5

# Cuckolding and Female Led Relationships

Since cuckolding is predominantly a female led activity, many couples who are enjoying this lifestyle are already in a Female Led Relationship. What you want to do is create a multi-partner experience while respecting the rules of the female led marriage or relationship. You may be accustomed to the woman being in-charge and leading the household. What the Queen decides must be respected and followed. If you have come to an agreement that it is beneficial for her to interact with the Bull with you watching, then that needs to be adhered. Maybe the Queen decides she wants you to participate, then this is what you will do. However, clear boundaries must be established for both of you and the Bull. Everything must be clearly explained to the Bull before engaging in anything to prevent any unwanted activity. If the Queen decides she wants to make the first move to start things off, then this must be adhered to. Men in an FLR must never take it upon themselves to do anything with cuckolding that was not authorized by the female. Since she will probably be the person engaging with a stranger, she needs to be careful and confident about how this is done.

I recall a scene from the movie *9½ Weeks*, which I always found disturbing. Mickey Rourke's character forces Kim Bassinger's character to engage in cuckolding against her will. While she tried to enjoy it for his sake, she was clearly not in control of the situation, which later affected her psychologically and created a sense of terror for all. I feel that it would have been much more enjoyable if she was a willing participant. Cuckolding should always be approached with great care and respect for all people involved. In the Female Led Relationship, the man is the supportive gentleman. You are supporting the Queen's interaction with the Bull. As part of that support, if she decides she wants you to get involved, then you can do so. But the female still leads. Now, some couples take it a step further in which the man wishes to experience the humiliation by getting locked up by his woman with her Bull while watching them. This can be requested, but again you will need to respect how your Queen wants to proceed with this. She selects the Bull, and she decides how to proceed. This makes it a much easier situation and less opportunity for disagreements.

Cuckolding needs to be a positive experience for you and your partner. Once again, this is cuckolding *Love & Obey* style, and not BDSM. Women rule, but with loving female authority and not malice. The idea is that both of you are in a Female Led Relationship and you are both in love. You both want to stay with each other in a long-term relationship. The woman in the relationship must successfully and ethically deal with having outside lovers and keeping her primary relationship strong. This is very challenging, so any decisions to embark on cuckolding must not be taken lightly.

Cuckolding can be an exciting part of a Female Led Relationship because as the supportive gentleman, you are allowing your Queen to do what will make her happy. It can be a very exciting activity for both of you to do together. Some men can be worried that they lose the Queen to the Bull, but this is usually not the case. A woman who is in a relationship with a loyal partner in a female led lifestyle is more likely to stay with the man who serves her. Many couples experience more passion and sex than ever before. This means more of these relationships last longer.

# CHAPTER 6

# Is Cuckolding the Same as Polyamory

People often confuse cuckolding with polyamory, but they are different. A polyamorous relationship (from the Greek poly, meaning "many," and Latin amor, meaning "love") is a non-monogamous relationship. The couple can have intimacy with multiple partners all the time, and it is an actual lifestyle. Miley Cyrus most recently made polyamory famous when she revealed that though she was married, she is openly polyamorous. What was even more shocking was that Miley indicated her partners can be men women, gay, straight or transgender, and she was even spotted kissing Kaitlyn Carter. Although these couples have the freedom to be non-monogamous, there are still rules laid out that are followed. A great example of this was in the movie *Savages*. All three characters lived together, and each man had sex with the main female character Ophelia, played by Blake Lively. Even the Mexican cartel characters criticized this type of living as "savage" compared to their way of killing and murdering associates in the cartel. The irony is pervasive in this movie, but it was a good portrayal of modern polyamory. The three were considered the family unit.

Cuckolding is not the same. While the woman has sex with a Bull, he is not part of the main family unit, and in general, cuckolding is not happening with a gay man or a transgender. Cuckolding is mainly about the sex or humiliation, but it does not involve living and inviting others into the family unit. Polyamory may be the choice of some couples, but as Miley discovered, it's not simple. Her polyamorous ways were not shared by her husband Liam Hemsworth, and it led to their separation and divorce earlier in 2020. Their split also highlighted an extremely important point in that both the man and woman must be on board with the lifestyle, otherwise there will be a great deal of conflict. I also personally feel that while cuckolding appears to be much more restrained and selective while retaining a strong bond in the main relationship, inviting and living with several people as part of the family unit represents a much more complicated situation to manage. Cuckolding can be one or two nights of fun, whereas polyamory often involves living with multiple people on a day-to-day basis. Two completely different scenarios not to be confused.

One of the first Polyamorous groups was the Kerista communities, which began in 1956 in New York and San Francisco by John Pelz Presmont, where a community was created to allow polyfidelity and swinging. The community promoted hippie principles of love and freedom—the idea that no one belonged to anyone. Anything goes. Good Vibes. Groups were arranged by Best Friend Identity Clusters and made up of several men and women who rotated around sleeping with each other on a schedule. So, on any given night, each man would be sleeping with a different woman and vice versa. Polyfidelity offered a number of obvious advantages over more traditional family and intimacy styles. It caters to the desires of those who like sexual variety, yet allows this to occur in the context of lasting, deep, meaningful relationships. This blend of spice and stability is very refreshing to people who, in other situations, have had to forfeit a stable home life in order to experience variety or vice versa. The problem of having unrealistic expectations of what one partner can provide that often occurs in two-adult families is solved; no one individual needs to be all things to anyone else. The Keristas were the first to coin the word "compersion," which meant "free from jealousy" and "happiness from another person's happiness." In the case of polyamory, compersion meant happiness from seeing your partner content in other relationships.

# CHAPTER 7

# How to Choose the Right Bull

The Bull is the man chosen to have sex with. He is the additional person who will be introduced into the cuckolding activity. His job is to satisfy the woman, so great care will be needed when choosing the right man. At the top of the list will be hygiene and safety. As difficult as it is to choose someone who is attractive and well-endowed, it will be important to insist on safety with all the precautions. While this can be a buzzkill, it might be wise to select a man who takes great pride in his health and appearance.

Marisa Rudder

The next challenge is to choose a man who is willing to join. The good news is that many men enjoy being asked to do cuckolding and below are some of the reasons.

## Why Do Men Want to Be Bulls?

Men have always had a deep fantasy about satisfying a woman's every need, and now a man as a Bull can get action without the deep commitment. Sometimes these relationships become so deep that all three become friends, so in a way the Bull gets to be part of the sex but not have the constraints of the relationship. The Bull is also satisfying the Queen, therefore, in many ways he is the star who has been brought into the relationship to spice it up. He may not necessarily be larger in size, but often he is more confident and able to satisfy the Queen. The position of Bull is perfect for non-committal men who want to have the titillating enjoyment of kinky sex without commitment.

Many couples get so carried away with the enjoyment of this fantasy that they rush into choosing a Bull who is unsuitable. One example is the best friend. This might seem logical since you both know him and probably like him, but a best friend is a problem for many reasons. First is being emotionally connected, which means you both want to remain friends with him. Should the cuckolding fail to work out, you

42

don't want harsh feelings and emotional ties. This can lead to a complete destruction of the friendship, and it can affect even your larger circle of friends. Another example is to choose someone from your gym. This again may seem like a logical choice, especially from the health aspect, but unless you want to take the chance of not being able to return to your gym or your Bull talking about the experience with others at the gym, it is best to refrain from choosing a Bull in a familiar and frequented place.

One alternative is dating sites. The advantage to this is that the Bull is already open to the idea, and you and your partner can meet with him anonymously with no real threat to your normal life. Online dating has become a part of normal life that this seems like a logical and practical choice. Of course, the same safeguards would apply, such as meeting in a public place.

## Interracial Cuckolding

For many couples, interracial cuckolding is a big deal. The white woman's white husband has a small cock, and they want a black man with a huge cock. Often it is a white man with a below average size penis who wants to watch his white wife get fucked with a big black cock. The contrast tends to be very arousing, as well as the idea that a black man is seen as being well-endowed, physically strong and capable. There is also the idea that cuckolding is one thing but interracial cuckolding is even more taboo, so breaking all the old school rules is sexually arousing for many people. There was once a period when blacks and whites were forbidden to mix, and it was even worse if a black man was found with a white man's wife.

Today, people are pushing the boundaries with almost everything, including interracial encounters, and women are a big part of this evolution. While engaging a black man for cuckolding adventures may seem enticing, it is important to approach this with care for all of you. Not everyone is open and it is necessary to discuss it at length and be respectful of anyone you engage from any nationality. People can feel disrespected when others make assumptions. I had this happen many times when I was approached because the man wanted to try something exotic. While it felt like a compliment at first, I grew to resent being treated like a dish someone wanted to try. If you are a black couple, this could also occur with wanting to get a Bull who is a white man. So, the same holds true. Be respectful of the person.

# CHAPTER 8

# What Are the Rules and Boundaries?

Couples engaging in cuckolding must have rules and boundaries that clearly define what occurs in the relationship, and these must be extended to include the Bull. One of the first rules to establish is *where* cuckolding will happen. Will it be at your house or the Bull's? Since your comfort is important and safety is mandatory, having it in an environment you all can handle is best. Some couples may choose a hotel room for complete anonymity. Not a bad choice. You can reserve it, and invite the Bull over. Everyone is safe, and you are not entering privately-owned areas. If this is not an option, then you can choose your guest bedroom when the kids are not around. Again, this way it's not in your private space. You can also choose your pool area, if the weather permits as it's sexy and also allows you to keep your personal spaces private. The idea is that since this is a new adventure, keeping it separate from your day-to-day life is recommended.

When you have decided to do cuckolding, it is important to set up clearly defined boundaries with you and your Queen first. How will it play out? Will only your Queen approach the Bull or will both of you? Will the Queen decide how it will play out and give you instructions or will you be participating right from the start? This is why a Female Led Relationship is beneficial because the woman makes the rules.

She decides on what will happen, and all you need to do is follow. Boundaries must also involve what happens if anyone becomes uncomfortable or wants to stop. It should be clearly established that everyone aborts immediately. Getting into arguments of jealous fits of rage should never occur. This keeps everything running smoothly. Maybe your Queen wants to stop. The appropriate and respectful response is to all agree. The Bull's state of mind must also be considered, and if he is unable to perform, you decide a respectful way to stop. At no time should anyone be made to feel pathetic or bad. You must prevent any chance of a fun situation to spiral out of control.

Another important point in boundaries is to discuss the importance of honesty. The bond between you and your woman must be maintained, and at no time should either of you engage with the Bull alone or without consent. The idea of cuckolding as opposed to cheating is the lying, hiding and secrecy that often occurs with infidelity. Maintaining trust is the biggest factor. Often in cheating, it is the dishonesty that does the most destruction to relationships, which is why the trust and the understanding to always be honest and open about cuckolding is the key. It should be understood that there will be no emotional ties with the Bull from either of you.

## Some of the Steps to Begin With

The best place to start is with open communication. Discuss everything very openly. What do you like, and what does she like? How do you see the activity unfolding? What is considered completely forbidden? What would you be open to exploring?

The next step is to spend some time talking about the fantasy, so that you can explore anything uncomfortable about it. Communication about everything is going to make things so much smoother. Decide on safe words to say in case you feel strange about a situation. Then it's time to go out and engage with people. Just spend some time talking about it or hanging out with others in a bar setting. Without directly engaging a single man, you could set up scenarios to approach a single man in a bar with the goal of solely getting experience for the both of you to feel comfortable even talking with a third. Maybe your Queen wants to dance with another man and flirt with him while you watch. This can be an easy way to determine how you and she feels about it.

One of my first experiences with this was when one of my ex-boyfriends encouraged me to dance with a friend of his. At first, I was a bit shocked that he did not care, and I was extremely uncomfortable with his aggressive flirtation in front of my boyfriend who had no issue with it. I later learned that it was something my boyfriend liked, and he and his friend were used to it. Needless to say, the relationship ended, but I learned that just dancing and flirting in a similar scenario was enough to determine if cuckolding will be right for you.

If you both cannot get past this step or there are signs of jealousy, you may not be ready. Getting comfortable with the process is imperative, and being OK if the first time does not go well. After each encounter, even at a bar, discuss your feelings about it openly. Discuss any hesitations and what can be done to resolve them. Maybe you did not like how she

48

positioned herself with a third and excluded you. Or you like that she took the initiative to approach a man, then inviting both of you to sit and chat. It is important to discuss everything and decide if cuckolding is worth pursuing. I can recall one of my ex-boyfriends asking me to be in an open relationship and me saying I was fine with it, when I was not ready to pursue anything at the time. I think it was my unwillingness to be honest, which eventually drove a rift between us.

The next step is to go online. Numerous dating sites are already set up for cuckolding with many mainstream ones having options to explore this. Spend time reading and looking at profiles and deciding together who would be suitable. Be respectful when you first approach someone and make the first dates a time to just meet and talk. The more comfortable you are with the Bull, the better it will be. Keep personal details to a minimum and always make sure everyone is onboard with safety and precautions.

Make some general rules and expectations for the night. For example, you may say to your partner, "Let's go out tonight with Dan to dinner, and afterwards we can come back, go in the hot tub and just start there. Nothing has to happen. It can just be a night of getting to know him and just have fun."

Later on, as you get more comfortable, you can have some sensual times in a hot tub with just kissing or allowing the Bull to feel her up. The Queen's decision about how far she is willing to go must be established, but there is no harm in starting with baby steps. The more smoothly each encounter goes, the better the turnout. Some couples progress with just fingering or use of sex toys only as the exploration continues. Then once everyone is on board, you can all plan for the full experience of the Bull having intercourse with your woman while you watch.

Some variations prior to intercourse could include you performing oral sex to your woman, then let her be fucked by the Bull. Whatever happens, she must make the rules, and you can decide if you agree. It's much more fun and inclusive for you to participate in some way, with the main act to be reserved for the woman with the Bull.

You should never feel ashamed if you are feeling jealousy. Jealousy is a powerful human emotion. It doesn't mean you're closed-minded or prudish. No matter how "cool" you are, jealousy is going to flare up. That doesn't mean "this kind of relationship isn't for you." Jealousy typically means you need some special attention. As partners in a significant relationship with someone, you must be willing to work through feelings. Opening up yourselves to new sexual experiences can bring on all sorts of feelings, and you must be allowed to experience them openly. Many couples go through this, and it is perfectly normal. The emotions are part of the thrill ride—the jealousy, the passion, the desire—are all wrapped up in your feelings and that's what makes the experience so exciting to everyone involved. You both also need to be respectful of the Bull and if there are any hesitations.

"Humans seem to have evolved to be primarily monogamous, with occasional cheating," stated University of Michigan psychology professor William McKibbin, PhD. As a result, about four percent of children worldwide are fathered by someone other than the man who believes he is the father, according to a meta-analysis published in the *Journal of Epidemiological Community Health* (Vol. 59, No. 9). That tendency allows females to have more genetic variety among their offspring, but for the cuckolded man, it is not good.

To defend against cuckoldry, men have developed a variety of behavioral and biological defenses, according to McKibbin. He also found that men at greater risk for cuckoldry, as measured by the proportion of time they'd spent away from their partners, became more interested in having sex with their partners. They also found their partners more attractive and engaged in "mate guarding" behavior. This result was independent of the amount of time since the couple last had sex, so it wasn't just the result of built-up desire—and it was moderated by how much a man trusted his mate not to cheat, McKibbin found. One such finding, in McKibbin's *Comparative Psychology* study reported that men at risk for cuckoldry were later more likely to pressure their partners into having sex. More sex in this case is not always better because it is driven by fear. In this case, the trust factor is also threatened, which could lead to issues long-term.

# CHAPTER **9**

# Creating a Cuckolding Agreement

A greements and contacts come in handy in business and can be very useful in relationships for the simple fact that humans are forgetful. So, to remind both parties of the rules, it may be a great idea to create a mini agreement together.

Start by answering questions such as:

- Are you interested in having open sexual experiences together, separately, or anything goes?

- What kinds of sexual fantasies thrill or excite you?

- What kinds of sexual fantasies create fear or anxiety in you?

- Is there a "line" that you do not want your partner to cross?

- What would be a relationship deal-breaker for you?

For example, a partner might say, "We are okay with us having sex with one special person or couple, but we are not okay with us having sex with unlimited people and couples."

- What is your dream of the perfect scenario for an open relationship?

- What are your risk thresholds for maintaining sexual, health and physical safety?

- What do you need from each other to maintain emotional comfort?

- How accessible do you want your primary partner to be if they're with an outside lover?

- How would you handle the sleeping arrangements and overnight experiences?

- Do you see outside experiences happening in your home and bedroom or do you see this happening in hotels?

- If you want to have experiences in your home, how do you deal with your children, if you have them?

- What kind of new partner are you looking for?

- How involved in our primary relationship do you want your outside partners to be; casual acquaintances, good friends, lovers and even domestic partners with us?

- What do your partners need so that they can deal with your desire to have sex right away with someone?

What communication rules will you set in place to maintain an open, healthy conversation around your outside affairs?

## The Love & Obey Agreement

Here is a sample of the Love & Obey Female Led Relationship Agreement that can serve as a guideline for your personalized non-monogamous "Openish" relationship.

**THIS LOVE & OBEY "OPENISH" FEMALE LED RELATIONSHIP AGREEMENT** is made and entered into on _____, by and between _____---, ("Primary Female") and _____, ("Primary Male"). Hereinafter referred to individually as the **"Primary Male"** and **"Primary Female"** and collectively as the **"Primary Partners."**

**WHEREAS,** the Primaries wish to enter into an open and non-monogamous relationship for the term of this Agreement and any extensions will be mutually agreed to by the Primaries.

## GRANT OF RIGHTS

On the terms provided herein, the **Primary Partners** hereby allow each other to enjoy an open and non-exclusive relationship and the Primaries accept such a relationship upon the terms listed below.

A. The **Primary Partners** will devote their best efforts to honoring the relationship and not acting in an anything goes manner. The Primaries will always ask permission before having an outside sexual experience and share the details of the experience with the other Primary afterwards;

B. The **Primary Partners** prefer inclusion and connection with the other parties and participation in sexual activities. However, if one of the **Primary Partners** is unavailable to connect or to be included or either Primary prefers the other not to be included, this will not prevent the other **Primary Partner** from moving forward solo;

a) The Primaries are permitted to engage in:

   1. **Casual Connections,** meaning one-time or sporadic hook-ups.

   2. **Committed Connections,** meaning an ongoing series of experiences with the same person that may occur regularly, for example, once a week or once a month.

   3. **Meaningful Connection,** meaning multiple visits per week and the potential for long term commitment;

a. New **Casual Connections, Committed Connections** or **Meaningful Connections** will initially be analyzed from the potential for inclusion of the **Primary Partners**. The **Primary Partners'** goal is to maximize time together with the other **Primary Partner**, to expand their sexual experiences together, and to maintain a happy Female Led Relationship together, and to build an expanded love and sexual experience that includes outside people;

b. We will only engage with outside partners who state their support and embrace the **Primary Partners'** original Female Led Relationship. Only outside connections who are giving positive and supporting energy will be discussed and considered as acceptable outside lovers. The **Primary Partners** will engage in any new potential connection with full disclosure of the **Primary Partners'** existence, and expect full acknowledgment from the new connection of their role as the **Primary Partners**;

c. Engage in any new potential connection with full disclosure of my **Primary Partners'** existence, and expect full acknowledgment from the new connection; and

d. **Casual Connections:** The physical line is drawn at nudity, flirting, kissing and manual stimulation. For safety and full disclosure purposes, we send the meeting locations to our **Primary Partner** for first-time connections.

e. **Committed Connections:** The initial physical line is set at kissing and manual stimulation, and progression to sexuality will be thoroughly discussed between the **Primary Partners**. Sexual dynamics will be adjusted to ensure physical safety of the **Primary Partners**. Permission to engage in sleeping overnight, oral and/or penetrative sex only when full medical STD test results have been exchanged to ensure full sexual and emotional safety. This is a sexual relationship that both **Primary Partners** believe is unlikely to evolve into a Meaningful Connection, or a full meaningful relationship.

f. **Sleeping Overnight:** Will be allowed once testing and safety concerns are satisfied to both the **Primary Partners'** satisfaction.

Overnight affairs are allowed when sleeping alone for a **Primary Partner** is approved and is guaranteed not to cause awkwardness, shamefulness or unhappiness if the other **Primary Partner** will not be involved.

g. **Communication:** Attempt to check in at least once during an exclusive overnight experience for reassurance, sharing as many or few details as desired by your other **Primary Partner**. A brief and loving voice message is exchanged before bed and again in the morning between the **Primary Partners**.

h. **Commitment and** respect are outwardly expressed for my **Primary Partner** by demonstrating a zero-tolerance policy for slut-shaming. We treat each other's desire to share intimacy with more than one person at a time with dignity. We recognize when each of us is emotional and show the **Primary Partner,** who is not having an outside connection, our consideration and appreciation for respecting our right to enjoy outside sexual experiences.

i. **Courtesy is** shown by consciously adding new partners into the relationship at a reasonable pace and maintaining an open and honest depth of sharing the experience. We show regard for the psychological impact of drastic life changes for our **Primary Male**, even though it is beyond his control. The **Primary Female** agrees to make a reasonable effort to respond to her **Primary Male** if they experience discomfort, even if it interferes with her own pleasurable experience. The **Primary Female** agrees to evaluate the gravity of interrupting her experience to address the **Primary Male's** discomfort.

j.  **Female Led Lifestyle:** The **Primary Male** is willing to face various degrees of self-discipline and discomfort to enable our **Primary Female's** freedom within our relationship, while still addressing my **Primary Male's** ego and its elimination, which takes time. work. Work to release **Primary Male** ego triggers and wounding of my **Primary Male's** pride, which no longer serves me or our Female Led Relationship. As the **Primary Male**, I will ask myself the following questions: Have I examined my why for this experience, my observations of it, and the reasons my emotions and needs are so uncomfortable? Am I still a **Primary Male** with a patriarchal male ego who wants to interrupt my Female leader's pleasure and fun?

k. **Male Aggression or Conflict: Primary Males** agree only to use non-violent communication to co-regulating and deal with the **Primary Female** leader when the **Primary Male** is struggling with the female outside sexual connections. **Primary Males** agree to express and discuss their negative feelings toward the **Primary Female are** ignored to avoid resentment and passive-aggressive **Primary Male** behavior. Allow the **Primary Male** to "Just say No!" and have the right to stop an outside female led connection for 72 hours. This time is to be used for the **Primary Male's** chance to explain and offer their heart-felt non-violent discussion of what is bothering and upsetting them. Both **Primary Partners** agree to share anything that they are tempted to hide from the other **Primary Partner** to enjoy fearless, shameless and guilt free outside sexual experiences. As the **Primary Male,** I will ask myself the following questions: Have I sat down with myself and explored all the avenues of self-resolution, so I can accept her outside lovers? Will waiting until after she has enjoyed her outside connection jeopardize our Female Led Relationship, or do I have to say "No!" And talk right now?

l. **Peer Pressure:** Prevent outside influence and judgment from friends, family, and outside lovers that will compromise or damage the integrity of our Female Led Relationship.

m. **Willingness to Stop:** Engaging in ongoing connections with unavailable monogamously married or committed people. The **Primary Female** is willing to re-organize her outside relationship to eliminate the **Primary Male's** fear or insecurity. The **Primary Male** is willing to engage the **Primary Female** to reopen any discussion and renegotiation. However, the **Primary Male** understands that he must be prepared for any outcome and accept the **Primary Female's** final decision with love and kindness. If I can't recall a particular agreement I had with my **Primary**

**Partner** and am in danger of transgressing, I will try to check in with my **Primary Partner** for clarity. The **Primary Female** agrees to abandon any philosophy of "I do everything only because it suits my fancy." Both **Primary Partners** consciously agree to communicate and accepted revision based on the discussion.

**IN WITNESS WHEREOF**, the Parties have executed this Agreement with the intention of being bound by it as of the date first above written.

The **Primary Female (Queen)**_____

Signature:                                    Date:

The **Primary Male (Supportive Gentleman)** _____

Signature:                                    Date:

Remember it is a guide for you and an agreement that can be revised as you go along, but trust me, it is necessary in this lifestyle. Although the agreement is not carved in stone, it should be specific, clear and comprehensive for you both and is helpful in dealing with any emotional crisis that arises, specifically when your primary partner—whether a wife, husband, girlfriend or boyfriend—knows you are going to be having sex with someone else besides them.

The agreement helps the spirit of freedom and allows you to experience the flow understanding more of the nuances of open relationship lifestyle. Remember this is only a guide for you, and you should adjust it based on your many life experiences. We all have different needs and our desires have evolved from different places. Don't be fixated on one way to live an open relationship, keep your mind open and the ideas flowing so you can enjoy this female led way of life. Female Led Relationships give the primary partners a safe lifestyle in which to explore their sexual fantasies. Our relationship isn't like a fortress; rather, it's an open estate that allows for visitors and new friends to stay and flow through.

# CHAPTER **10**

# The First Cuckolding Encounter

Now that all of the discussion, practice and agreement has happened, it's now time to get to your first encounter. This is likely to have lots of excitement and anticipation with it. Ensure you are equipped with your safety items—condoms, birth control, etc. You may want to have a set of sheets set aside specifically for this. Even better if it happens in a hotel room or a place separate from your main home. If you have kids, you want to ensure they are not exposed in any way to this activity.

Ideally, it's best to set schedules and choose a time to meet. It may be a good idea to meet at a restaurant or bar. You should both try to dress to impress in something that is applicable to the act. If your Queen wants to have extra outfits or sex toys, she can pack these things. Personal hygiene is of the utmost importance, which is why a hotel room works so you have access to a bathroom. If you decide to have it in your home, it might be wise to designate a specific room so you can set it up, with mood and ambiance of your choosing. Pools, hot tubs, Jacuzzis, beachfront with access to a beach or a penthouse suite overlooking the city are all wonderful areas to reserve for the first encounter.

When you first get to the place, start with getting everyone comfortable. Have some drinks; listen to music. You can begin with some light play with your Queen. Just engage slowly and sexy to get everyone in the mood. Then you can all move to the bedroom. If your Queen has decided you will watch, go to your chair and allow her to lead.

She should already have determined how she wants to have intercourse and just allow things to unfold. Be open and stick to your established boundaries. No one should go off script. It may be wise to make the first encounter short. Be aware of how you feel during the first time so you can decide if it will happen in the future. The key is to enjoy the moment. Focus on your Queen and her enjoyment. Refrain from intervening unless she specifically allows you to jump in. Then only focus your attention on her. The more comfortable you all get, the better things will flow. Once the encounter is done, the Bull can leave, and you both can continue together, cuddle or talk. Take showers or just unwind. It is important to have a period of togetherness after the act.

# CHAPTER **11**

# Creating Perfect Cuckolding Scenarios

N ow that you have successfully accomplished your first encounter, there are so many ways to make the follow up so much better.

Here are a few suggestions:

## 1. *Change Up the Locations*

Change your venue—maybe you meet at a club and dance and flirt, then hit the hot tub, or maybe you have dinner before going to a hotel room. Las Vegas has several options for seductive hotels to put you in the mood. Los Angeles and NYC also offer lots of options. Going on vacations could be another exciting way to add adventure. Desire Resort in Mexico is already set up for fetishes and all sorts of alternative lifestyles. Plus, you can be assured that everyone there is interested in variety. I recently read about a town I thought was super vanilla, but Toronto has a sex hotel complete with a sex menu. Keep the fantasy alive with lots of variety.

## 2. Set Up a Playroom

Who can forget the sumptuous playroom in *Fifty shades of Grey*? Christian Grey knows how to create the perfect playroom with luxurious red carpeting and high-quality leather furniture. Many couples have created similar playrooms, which are kept locked and private as Mommy and Daddy's special room and can be filled with all sorts of adult toys to use with your Bull. Many couples have added swings, sex cushions and BDSM crosses with whips to add some light bondage to the experience. The idea is to make it fun and fantastical as possible.

## 3. Attend Formal Fetish Parties

One of my most memorable times was to be invited to a party straight out of the movie *Eyes Wide Shut* complete with mansion, costumes and passwords. It was unbelievable. The advantage is that you meet people who are in the lifestyle and may be open to join you on your cuckolding adventure. This can not only spice up your relationship with new ideas but it can help you to find more than one suitable bull. These parties often come with their own firm rules and opportunities to explore.

## 4. Add Costumes

There is a reason we love Halloween, and people enjoy dressing up. Costumes during sex is no different and allows you to be someone else, enhancing the fantasy. You and your Queen can dress up or you can watch while she and the Bull use costumes. It is important to keep the sexiness alive. At a minimum, your Queen should be in sexy lingerie. Refrain from wearing normal underwear like you in "tighty whities" and she in granny panties. I have had to suggest to many couples the importance of keeping it sexy. Yes, you want to be comfortable but sweat pants and sweat shirts don't cut it when you are trying to have an adventure. You as a doctor and she as the nurse with the Bull as the patient is far more exciting. Costumes also help to distinguish between fun encounters and love-making sessions with your Queen. Costumes are great for both and add lots of variety.

## 5. Use a Cock Cage

A cock cage is the device and comes complete with a lock to fasten the man's penis up. Male chastity devices are usually "cock cages" or "penis cages" that are made from metal or plastic, depending on the design. These cages imprison the penis, making it impossible for men to masturbate, have sex, or get a full erection. This allows the couple to engage in chastity in which the woman is going to control the man's penis and his ability to orgasm. During cuckolding, the woman is in control and her dominance extends to you and the Bull. Men in chastity report feelings of excitement and adventure.

Allowing your woman to put you in chastity can add to the excitement of the experience. Some men enjoy long-term male chastity, wearing a penis cage for months at a time until the woman tells them they're allowed to take it off. Others wear their cock cage for a few hours or days as a way to prove loyalty to their spouse or a sexual partner. The anticipation of sex and heightened arousal that this builds up over time can cause the eventual release of sperm to be explosive and heightened. This is how the excitement is built as you are held in chastity, allowing your woman supreme power to do what she wishes. There is no greater devotion.

## 6. *Be Spontaneous*

Maybe you are out at a party, bar or on vacation. Be spontaneous. You could strike up a conversation, do some flirting, go to a sexy after-hours spot or a strip club. Sometimes being spontaneous and naughty can lead to some very exciting moments. Check out a sex club randomly one night. Just opening your mind can lead to some very exciting cuckolding adventures.

## 7. *Go on an Adult Vacation*

One of the best ways to do cuckolding with anonymity is to go on adult vacations. Today, there are a number of these resorts set up specifically for adventurous couples looking for exploration. Resorts like Desire, Maya Riviera in Mexico and The Ranch in Las Vegas are some places that can provide this type of experience. The advantage of the resort is it is anonymous but most people there are in the lifestyle.

# CHAPTER **12**

# How to Deal with Hesitations

There may be a situation where you or your Queen have hesitations about cuckolding. Many men don't always feel confident about allowing their woman to engage with another man, and there is the fear that she will be stolen away and become obsessed with the bull. This was the reason to refrain from engaging with a friend or someone with an emotional connection. In a Female Led Relationship, the Queen makes the decision and you must follow her rules. However, you and your Queen should come to an understanding about how cuckolding will enrich your current relationship and assess the reasons you want to add it to your life.

## How to Introduce Cuckolding?

Sometimes it is the man who must try to introduce it to the Queen. Begin by introducing the idea as a way to spice things up and have some adventure. You can explain that you will enjoy voyeurism and it's something you want to explore safely. Explain that the experience would be for her pleasure and you only want her happiness.

Many modern women will be open since it naturally benefits them. Who doesn't want a very attractive man worshipping you once in a while? Some women now have a voracious appetite for sex, so she can feel happy that it is her needs that are being satisfied. I can recall the countless nights when I felt empty and unsatisfied with the sex and longed for more. But my upbringing and religious conditioning forbid me to ever explore these alternatives. You can assure her that it's not shameful or wrong, as long as you both can reach an agreement. It's perfectly OK for a woman to explore her sexuality with her body that she owns and controls. It is outdated for men to think that they own a woman's body. The most important point is to communicate and talk about the topic at length before beginning. Start fantasizing with him so he can think about how you would want it to unfold and get turned on. You can get her to start by imagining that the other man is present during sex with her at first. If it turns both of you on, then you can figure out if it's right for you.

Just talking about it will be a huge turn on for both of you. Describing how it might happen and what would go on is a great initial way to open up about it. Discussing fantasies together can add to the excitement by foreshadowing what is about to happen and you both formulate the perfect scenario. Go out and start immersing her in the possibilities of this type of relationship. Talk, flirt, dance and get her accustomed to places where there may be alternative lifestyles occurring. There are lots of fetish clubs around that you can attend where you both can meet people in the lifestyle. The most important thing to do with your woman is to assure her that you are still 100 percent committed to her. Make a promise that whatever you do with cuckolding is done together with an awareness of her needs.

Spend time asking what she likes. When my partner was interested in my fantasies and what turned me on, I was shy at first to talk about it but, once I began to get comfortable with it, the flood gates opened. All I wanted to do was try new things. You get hooked, and women who are generally much more conservative in their experiences can begin to open up and have fun.

What has to be emphasized is that cuckolding, and any other alternative lifestyle activity, should be something you always do together. Your Queen is not expected to go out and do this on her own. Nor should she. Cuckolding should be approached as the extra activity you do together.

# CHAPTER **13**

# Avoid Common Pitfalls

As with anything new worth exploring, cuckolding can have some pitfalls that you and your Queen will need to avoid. During Lehmiller's interview with CNN, he stated, "We found several personality factors that predict more positive experiences acting on cuckolding fantasies. For those who have a lot of relationship anxiety or abandonment issues, who lack intimacy and communication, and who aren't careful, detail-oriented planners, acting on a consensual non-monogamy fantasy could very well be a negative experience."

This raises the important issues of avoiding common pitfalls. I recently had a client who we will name Bob. His name has been changed to protect his privacy. Bob has been in a Female Led Relationship for about two years. He does everything he is supposed to do, but now his wife has instructed that he partake in cuckolding. Bob wants to be supportive but he has major feelings of anxiety about having to see his wife with another man and possibly be forming a bond with the bull. One of the ways that Bob deals with the anxiety is by lashing out at his wife but he refuses to be truthful with her, which is a common issue couples face. No one wants to be the buzzkill, and no one wants to admit that there is an issue. First of all, Bob is in a relationship, so out of respect, there should be honest communication. Then, secondly, Bob needs to raise his issues with his Queen and discuss it openly. This is where the boundaries come in. If Bob could get assurances that the relationship will be sound and she remains bonded to him, it will ease his anxiety. So, this is a very good example of a common feeling and how to get around it.

Communication is the key. Today, Bob and his wife have successfully had a few cuckolding encounters and he reported that his relationship has never been better. He has honest communication with this wife and it has helped them to get past some of the original hesitations.

Another common pitfall is inviting a friend to join in during cuckolding. Let's face it, we are human, and we love our friends and quite often couples can place a great deal of trust in a friend. So, I recently met Laura and Dan (names have been changed) who have been married for five years, and recently Dan was discussing with his friend Luke about boredom setting in and that he and Laura wanted to try cuckolding. Dan admitted that he wanted an easy way of trying it out and Luke offered to be the Bull. They successfully had two encounters and Luke gets a girlfriend. Then one night while at dinner, it slips out that Luke had sex with Laura while Dan watched, causing shock in the other people at the table, Luke's girlfriend stormed out and Laura and Dan were left feeling panicked and embarrassed to the point where they could no longer engage with their friends. This represents yet another pitfall involving friends and inviting them into your home for cuckolding adventures.

Another pitfall is to get carried away with the fantasy that you both forget the primary relationship. After your cuckolding encounter, it is extremely important to share the experience with your Queen and for you both to discuss your likes and dislikes about it. You both also need to spend some time together for intimate times and sex. Some couples reconnect with oral sex or love-making worship sessions. This is crucial to keep the bond and the strength of the main relationship alive. It helps to ensure you both feel connected in your primary relationship. It helps to keep cuckolding as the side adventure you have from time to time. At no point should you or your partner form an emotional bond with the bull. He is not part of the primary relationship.

Psychologist Lisa Firestone said, "When it comes to their intimate relationships, couples can make any decision they want about monogamy, as long as this decision is mutually agreed upon by both partners." Emotional risk is something else to consider. Even if you're completely on board at the start, feelings can change at any time. One person may decide they want to stop, the cuck may begin to experience more jealousy than he bargained for, or one or both of the people hooking up could become too attached. Cuckolding requires complete honesty from everyone involved every step of the way. Communicate frequently to make sure you're all still on the same page. If anyone is uncomfortable or unsure, or if anything feels off, stop and figure out what to do next.

Let's be honest, open relationships and cuckolding are not without their share of controversy. Most of the male critics try to paint cuckolding as a fancy way of allowing wives to cheat. While I understand the need to criticize it as it threatens patriarchal and misogynist views of a monogamous male led relationship, I do not agree with their attempts at trying to squash free speech and discussion about this subject. And despite what some men say, there are examples of how cuckolding is benefiting relationships around the world. You might not think that an open relationship (cuckolding, threesomes, hotwifing and group sex) would bring two people closer, but in my research, many couples reported strong feelings of connection after experience sex with someone outside the two of them. Many also reported more intimacy and appreciation for their partners. There were reports of more trust and openness because after a shared open relationship experience, nothing has to remain secretive or in the dark ever again. This openness often leads to a renewed sense of trust, closeness and togetherness, all of which are all hugely beneficial for the long-term health of any relationship.

Another big plus was that couples reported much more passionate sex when they were alone together because of their outside experience. One of the biggest complaints of most relationships is the lack of sex, the decline in the quality of sex and overall boredom with sex. Most couples who practice open relationships have been together for years, and quite often the cuckolding, threesomes or more comes to help keep the excitement alive even when the couple is just by themselves. Most people don't have outside relationships all the time, typically people have one, once in a while. Maybe that is once a month, once a quarter or even once a year.

However, that sexual freedom is with you every day and makes sex with your primary partner so much more exciting.

Perhaps you discuss to get in the mood, or even while you are having sex with each other. Let's face it, human beings are always searching for more. So, more excitement in a relationship is essential. Open relationships breathe new and exciting life into a relationship that, while loving and committed, may feel a bit boring and stale. The voyeuristic and taboo nature of cuckolding—or whatever you have chosen to do—creates a cool, kinky vibe for some couples and opens endless possibilities for exciting and highly satisfying sexual experiences together.

Overall, women reported feeling more sexually fulfilled and satisfied than ever before, especially in cuckolding relationships. Variety is the spice of life, and cuckolding offers ample opportunity for women to enjoy a selection of enthusiastic sexual partners. Some of these men may do things that their husband or boyfriend just do not do well and they may fulfill additional sexual fantasies and desires, like being dominated, or having sex with a man with a substantially larger penis. But it doesn't end with cuckolding; a threesome is the most common sexual fantasy in Americas, according to many surveys' individuals aged 18 to 87, 95 percent of men and 87 percent of women said they had fantasized about sex with multiple partners. Studies in North America have established that about one in every five people or 20 percent of people have engaged in some form of multiple partner relationship at some point in their lives and that number is growing.

If there's one thing open relationships and cuckolding has shown us, it's that a pretty significant percentage of the population is clearly drawn to non-monogamous relationships, yet a much smaller percentage is willing to admit it. For the people who choose to engage in these types of non-monogamous activities, is it better to come to an agreement with their partner or to sneak around and deceive. Open relationships can work, but how can two people, alone in their romantic union, engage in this lifestyle that is considered taboo? That is the challenge.

For any relationship to work, there are certain fundamental qualities to be aware of. In an open relationship, in which a couple chooses not to hide or to allow infidelity, it is all the more important to encourage honest communication and healthy ways of handling emotions like jealousy, victimization or a desire to control.

Some of the elements you'll want to avoid if you want to keep things close, consistent and exciting between you and your partner is to include dishonesty and fear. Irreparable damage is done when there is dishonesty in a relationship and it is finally discovered. Lying leads to pain that cannot be undone. Dr. Firestone cites research that has shown unfaithful individuals are less likely to practice safe sex than people in open relationships. This act of deception thus poses both a physical and emotional threat to their partner.

She stated, "Whatever their decision is regarding monogamy, if two people want their relationship to stay strong, they must strive to be open and truthful and to ensure their actions always match their words." An open relationship without honesty is disastrous and deception is likely to lead to the same feelings of hurt and distrust. We may not be able to control our attractions, but we can control how we behave and how we deal with these feelings. Being open with our partner and encouraging them to be open with us will inspire an atmosphere of honesty.

Fear is another major issue. Fear of intimacy and fear of losing your partner to this new activity, cuckolding. Fear is a tremendous problem because it can make us paralyzed in a relationship. Couples find it difficult to get past the feeling that they could lose one another and grow apart. Maybe you think your Queen will get swept away by the Bull so you begin to have and harbor these fears. What makes this even more complicated is the fact that this fear can sit below the surface, so it isn't entirely conscious. Instead of thinking, "I'm scared of losing her" we will have thoughts like, "She is too good for me. I can't make this kind of commitment right now. I don't want to get hurt when she leaves."

Fear can leave a lasting destructive imprint on what could have been a fun activity so it is important to get it out in the open and discuss it openly. Reassuring each other through this process is vital. If you're interested in cuckolding or an open relationship, you may want to determine why. Are you interested in sexual freedom only or is there something missing from my current relationship and am I just moving away from my partner? No matter what type of relationship you are in when you are engaging in cuckolding, you'll have to get to know and challenge your own fears. These fears often come from old feelings of hurt, rejection or loss. It is important to deal with the underlying reasons for wanting to do this, so that it is clear you both are doing it for the right reasons.

# CHAPTER **14**

# Practicing Safe Sex

E nsuring safe sex is extremely important at all times during cuckolding. There is nothing worse than your partner, you or the bull, ending up with a sexually transmitted disease STD. STDs are sexually transmitted diseases. This means they are most often— but not exclusively—spread by sexual intercourse. HIV, chlamydia, genital herpes, genital warts, gonorrhea, some forms of hepatitis, syphilis, and trichomoniasis are considered an STD. It goes without saying that no encounter should ever involve the omission of a condom and other safeguards. Using a condom correctly every time you have sex can help you avoid STDs. Condoms lessen the risk of infection for all STDs. The failure of condoms to protect against STD/HIV transmission usually results from inconsistent or incorrect use, rather than product failure.

- Inconsistent or nonuse can lead to STD acquisition because transmission can occur with a single sex act with an infected partner.

- Incorrect *use* diminishes the protective effect of condoms by leading to condom breakage, slippage, or leakage. Incorrect use more commonly entails a failure to use condoms *throughout the entire* sex act, from start (of sexual contact) to finish (after ejaculation).

These are some suggestions to ensure proper use:

- A new condom should be used for every act of vaginal, anal and oral sex throughout the entire sex act (from start to finish). Before any genital contact, put the condom on the tip of the erect penis with the rolled side out.

- If the condom does not have a reservoir tip, pinch the tip enough to leave a half-inch space for semen to collect. Holding the tip, unroll the condom all the way to the base of the erect penis.

- After ejaculation and before the penis gets soft, grip the rim of the condom and carefully withdraw. Then gently pull the condom off the penis, making sure that semen doesn't spill out.

- Wrap the condom in a tissue and throw it in the trash where others won't handle it.

- If you feel the condom break at any point during sexual activity, stop immediately, withdraw, remove the broken condom, and put on a new condom.

- Ensure that adequate lubrication is used during vaginal and anal sex, which might require water-based lubricants. Oil-based lubricants (e.g., petroleum jelly, shortening, mineral oil, massage oils, body lotions, and cooking oil) should not be used because they can weaken latex, causing breakage.

You both may want to get tested so that you can offer evidence of being clean and healthy. You may want to request this of the bull as well, so everyone feels safe. It may also be warranted to have a discussion of exclusivity with the bull. Maybe it can be decided that if he is having sex with your wife, he reserves himself, at least for that time period to only be with you both. This may introduce pressure and a bit of buzzkill, but if safety is your highest concern, it cannot be avoided.

Your Queen will need to ensure that she is protected as well against pregnancy. It is interesting how in history, cuckolding was criticized for the fact that it involved an adulterous man who would often be bearing another man's child. Today, modern cuckolding does not have to have this unpleasant consequence especially if the right safeguards are taken.

# CHAPTER **15**

# Why Do Couples Crave Open Relationships?

onduct a couple of searches on Google, and you will see cuckolding has 150,000 people searching a month. Threesomes has about 600,000 searches and polyamory has about 125,000. All of these point to a strong interest in open relationships. But why? Couples reported strong feelings of connection after experience sex with someone outside the two of them. Many also reported more intimacy and appreciation for their partners. There were reports of more trust and openness because after a shared open relationship experience, nothing has to remain secretive or in the dark ever again. This openness often leads to a renewed sense of trust, closeness and togetherness, which are all hugely beneficial for the long-term health of any relationship.

Another big plus is that couples reported much more passionate sex when they were alone together because of their outside experience. One of the biggest complaints of most relationships is the lack of sex, the decline in the quality of sex and overall boredom with sex. Most couples who practice open relationships have been together for years, and quite often the cuckolding, threesomes or more comes to help keep the excitement alive even when the couple is just by themselves. Most people don't have outside relationships all the time, and typically people have one, once in a while. Maybe that is once a month, once a quarter or even once a year.

However, that sexual freedom is with you every day and makes the sex you have with your primary partner so much more exciting. Perhaps you talk about it to get in the mood, or even while you are having sex with each other. Let's face it, human beings are always searching for more. So, more excitement in a relationship is important. As mentioned, open relationships breathe new and exciting life into a relationship that, while loving and committed, may feel a bit boring and stale. The voyeuristic and taboo nature of cuckolding, or whatever you have chosen to do, creates a cool kinky vibe for some couples and opens endless possibilities for exhilarating sexual experiences together.

In addition, Scientists Ellen Berscheid and Elaine Walster suggest that there are two types of love, one that is based more on passion and another that is more about companionship. Passionate love has always been thought to fizzle out fast or become less fiery, more like friendship. You hear of the phrase, "Honeymoon is over." Relationships become less exciting.

However, companionship love, though marked by commitment, intimacy, and a sharing of interests tends to be less intense and can lack elements of sexual desire and attraction. Perhaps as a result, this type of love tends to be only moderately satisfying for individuals in relationships, leading them to want to spice up the relationship and pursue non-monogamy.

One misconception is that cuckolding can fix problems in a relationship. This is generally not the case and it may probably make it worse, if it's in trouble already. Fix your primary relationship first, and make sure it's working, or you are setting yourself up for failure. Don't expect someone else to put in the sexual and emotional labor to fix your primary relationship; you need to do it for yourself. Open relationships are not there to fill the gaps in your primary relationship that aren't thriving. Outside connections are not a means of outsourcing relationship labor to repair your problems. It's about creating an entirely new connection with someone else that hopefully enriches your primary relationship and expands your life experiences.

Another point is that some couples use cuckolding as a way to get around the "no cheating" rule. An open relationship is not the same as cheating. That means you don't have a sexual relationship or a romantic relationship without getting approval and full agreement from your partner. There will be the temptation to get emotionally involved with the bull and want extra time with him. This must be avoided. Cheating and sneaking around without informing your partner is cheating and can lead to disaster. It's really easy to get lopsided in an open relationship. When you get a new toy, sometimes you forget about your old favorite toy and you get carried away with the 'newness' of it all. But any kind of distrust or dishonesty can lead to destruction of the relationship and the marriage.

Threesomes, swinging and group sex is also not cuckolding and should not be lumped into the same group. The main difference with these other forms of open relationships is that it no longer is an intimate connection for you and your woman. In threesomes, couples engage with a man or woman equally. While this is a popular alternative it is not cuckolding where generally only your woman is engaging with the Bull. While cuckolding may be the decision of your Queen in a Female Led Relationship, threesomes can be something you introduce. Many men do enjoy threesomes where it's either another woman is joining in with you and your Queen or another man is invited. What is missing from this is the voyeur aspect and the expectation of full participation. You don't just get to watch on the sidelines. Swinging is yet another form and this involves swapping partners with another couple. Again, not the same as cuckolding. Seventeen percent of younger Americans say they have had sexual contact with other people with the consent of their partner compared to only three percent of over-65s who said the same.

This may be due to the rise in consensual non-monogamous relationship practices, like swinging where it is estimated that 2.35 percent of Americans currently self-identify as swingers and 4.76 percent had identified as swingers at some point in their lifetime. Finally, group sex when any number of people can be having sex at the same time with you and your partner. This will lack the intimacy of cuckolding and is again completely different.

# CHAPTER **16**

# How to Deal with Disagreements

I t is perfectly normal to have disagreements when exploring cuckolding and other types of alternative relationships. You and your Queen may experience jealousy or you may disagree on how the cuckolding experience unfolds. You may not want her to perform certain acts or on how many times it should be done.

The first thing to realize is that disagreements are normal and it is best to discuss them in an open fashion. One suggestion was that after each encounter, you discuss what happened and what should not happen. During these sessions it's important to be honest about feelings. If there was jealousy, get it out in the open and decide whether you should continue or not.

There may be times where you may not have agreed with what the Bull did. Again, open conversation with your Queen and the Bull is needed and should not be underestimated. In general, the Queen makes the decisions on how and what should be done, so you will want to allow her to be in charge. This takes the pressure off you and allows you to just enjoy the experience. Try to refrain from being too critical but review the rules and boundaries. The idea is that cuckolding is just an activity you add to your life; it is not your entire life and should be treated as such.

## Here are some key concerns to discuss:

- ✓ Are you enjoying the sexual experiences?

- ✓ Are you interested in exploring together or alone?

- ✓ What other kinds of sexual fantasies can we explore?

- ✓ What kinds of sexual fantasies are off limits?

- ✓ Is there a "line" that you do not want me to cross?

- ✓ What is your dream of the perfect cuckolding experience?

✓ Is there anything we should not do in cuckolding?

✓ How do you feel emotionally?

✓ Do you feel any jealousy?

✓ How many times a month is it healthy to do cuckolding?

✓ Should we remain friends with the Bull?

✓ What do we do when it's time to move on?

✓ What happens if we are not in agreement about this lifestyle?

✓ How do we handle our kids?

✓ How often should we talk about matters?

✓ Should I be more submissive?

✓ Should you be more demanding?

Our early experiences in relationships, starting with the ones we had with our parents or primary caretakers, heavily influence the psychological defenses we form and often face throughout our lives. These defenses may have been strategies we adopted to survive less than ideal conditions in our childhood. These adaptations may have helped us as kids, but they can go on to hurt us in our adult relationships.

Oftentimes, when we first fall in love, we are in an undefended state in which we are more open to another person. However, as we get closer, we may experience certain fears around intimacy and fall back to our old defenses. We may become more critical and guarded or become more anxious and controlling depending on our defense system. In addition, we may even be attracted to people who are likely to hurt us in the very same ways we were hurt as children. So, you and your Queen are dealing with all of this while exploring this new lifestyle.

One thing you will learn in an open relationship is to listen to what your partner says, even if it is challenging or frightening. You will learn to accept discomfort and go with it. Nobody said this was going to be the path of least resistance, in fact it is challenging, but can also be very rewarding. This approach will not necessarily protect you from being hurt. We often feel fireworks with people whose defenses fit with ours and who reaffirm old, familiar, often unpleasant ways of feeling about ourselves and others. While we may feel passion and excitement in the initial stages of these relationships, our defenses will often eventually get in the way, as we find ourselves either becoming more and more distant or increasingly pursuing our partner in ways that trigger their own defense system.

There are certain things that need to happen in order for an open relationship to be a healthy and happy experience. I believe there are essential things which must be done in any relationship. Psychologist Dr. Lisa Firestone found that "some essential characteristics that fit the description of a loving relationship include expressions of affection, both physical and emotional, a wish to offer pleasure and satisfaction to another, tenderness, compassion, and sensitivity to the needs of the other, a desire for shared activities and pursuits, an appropriate level of sharing of one's possessions, an ongoing, honest exchange of personal feelings and the process of offering concern, comfort, and outward assistance for the loved one's aspirations." If you and your Queen commit to these as principles, you both will be much more likely to stay in touch with your loving feelings and keep passion, attraction, respect, and admiration as living forces in your relationship.

You need to be extremely honest about feelings of jealousy. Jealousy is a natural human emotion. Yet, the way we use it can be very destructive. Dr Firestone stated, "Lurking behind the paranoia toward our partners, or the criticisms toward a perceived third-party threat, are often critical thoughts toward ourselves." She finds that a person's "critical inner voice" can bombard his or her mind with harmful suspicions and accusations that fuel feelings of jealousy. She frequently finds that what people are telling themselves about what's going on with their partner is often a lot worse than what is actually going on. It is important to discuss it openly with your Queen.

If you are scared, worried, angry, upset, say it. Disagreements erupt when there is a perceived feeling of distrust. Even when our worst fears materialize and we learn of a partner's affair, we frequently react by directing anger at ourselves for being "foolish, unlovable, ruined or unwanted." These shaming attitudes toward ourselves and our partner can breed an environment of distrust. If a healthy relationship must be built on honesty and trust, then jealousy has to be kept in check. The first way to do this is to own our emotions and deal with our inner critic rather than allowing it to poison our relationship. We should work hard to be vulnerable and be open to our partner, and to offer our trust and support for their independence and individuality. This doesn't mean we have to agree to an open relationship. It just means working on having open communication and trying not to allow our inner critic to overtake us and drive our behavior.

Anxiety is something else that can lead to disagreements. You and your Queen may be happily engaging in cuckolding but you begin to feel anxious that your relationship could fall apart. Anxiety can lead us to create distance between ourselves and our partner. At its worst, our anxiety can even push us to give up on love altogether. Being in a relationship and falling in love challenges us in numerous ways we don't expect. The more we value someone else, the more we stand to lose. On many levels, both conscious and unconscious, we become scared of being hurt.

When we are in relationships, it isn't just the things that go on between us and our partner that make us anxious.; it's the things we tell ourselves about what's going on. This is called "the critical voice." This critical inner voice makes us turn against ourselves and the people close to us. It can promote hostile, paranoid and suspicious thinking that lowers our self-esteem and drives unhealthy levels of distrust, defensiveness, jealousy and anxiety. Basically, it feeds us a consistent stream of thoughts that undermine our happiness and make us worry about our relationship, rather than just enjoying it.

The issue with anxiety and having open relationships is the added factors to deal with, which may not be in the open because neither you nor your partner wants to kill the vibe. If you suppress the feelings of anxiety, you could start to act out in destructive ways, making nasty comments or becoming childish or parental toward our significant other. If it continues, you've completely shifted the dynamic between you. Instead of enjoying the time you have together, you may waste an entire night feeling withdrawn and upset with each other. You've now effectively forced the distance you initially feared. The critical inner voice tends to terrorize and catastrophize reality. It can rouse serious spells of anxiety about dynamics that don't exist and threats that aren't even tangible.

Know what you want in your ideal openish relationship. What do you think cuckolding will bring to your life? What challenges do you imagine you will face and can you handle them? Do you have enough time for multiple partners? Do you want to have the time, energy and availability, for more people? What does your Queen want, desire and are you looking for the same sort of openish relationship? Are you open to doing what she wants, even if you don't get what you want? The defenses we form from the critical voices we hear are based on our own unique experiences and adaptations. When we feel anxious or insecure, some of us have a tendency to become clingy and desperate in our actions. We may feel possessive or controlling toward our partner in response.

Conversely, some of us will feel easily intruded on in our relationships. We may retreat from our partners, detach from our feelings of desire. We may act out by being aloof, distant or guarded. This behavior can lead to disagreements that threaten the bond of the primary relationship. That study, published in the *Journal of Family Psychology*, highlights the fact that the way you engage with your partner affects your overall well-being in many ways. How you treat your partner will affect how well you communicate. Creating and maintaining a sustaining intimate relationship isn't easy. But it is something you can practice. You and your partner can examine and reveal how you each experience your own self within the relationship: How do you see your own life "evolution" over the years? Are you in sync with each other's vision of life together? If there are gaps, how will you address and deal with them? Answering these questions can help with disagreements. Psychologist Douglas LaBier talks about "radical transparency," which can help couples assess such questions openly and honestly; this includes the following description of the two parts of radical transparency:

- Being open and revealing about yourself to your partner. This means letting go of inhibitions or defensive feelings you might be harboring about what you haven't revealed, and also acknowledging your reluctance to do so.

- Being open and receptive to *your partner's* reality—his or her feelings, wishes, desires, fears—and differences from yourself. It means openly encouraging your partner to express these to you.

LaBier believes that radical transparency can put you on the path to strengthening the foundation of your relationship, which can go a long way to reducing disagreements.

Studies show that stress can arise in relationships when partners experience conflicting goals, motives and preferences. Common sources of conflict involve unmet expectations, intimacy, time spent together, financial difficulties, discrepancies in equity and power, domestic and family responsibilities, parenting, jealousy, bad habits and more. Unresolved conflicts and the tension associated with conflict put even the most satisfying relationship at risk.

Moreover, managing and resolving conflict is difficult, and can itself be a significant source of stress. Indeed, one of the most pressing problems couples identify is how to communicate while resolving their disagreements, and relationship therapists agree that dysfunctional communication is the most damaging and difficult to treat a relationship problem. Identifying what constitutes effective communication during conflict is thus critical to help couples resolve problems and sustain their relationships.

# CHAPTER **17**

# Keep the Primary
# Relationship Alive

When people complain about being bored in their relationship, they often cite being stuck in a rut or routine. Then there is the worry about how to keep the relationship alive. They may feel a sudden desire for novelty and assume that novelty can only come from a new partner. One of the biggest issues with cuckolding is the tendency for the primary relationship to begin to break down. All the focus goes to the cuckolding experience, and it is possible for the primary relationship to become mundane and insignificant. Here are a few tips on how to keep the primary relationship between you and your Queen strong:

### Re-enforce Your Relationship Daily

Remind her of the love you both feel daily. Kiss, hug, greet her as the Queen and don't allow the relationship to take a backseat. In our busy world we tend to place other matters above the relationship and only when going out do we make a big deal. We make excuses for being busy, tired, or just not in the mood. Now more than ever, you both will need to spend time on the relationship.

### Take Care of Your Health and Fitness

Often so much is going on that we barely have time to worry about upkeep of our health and fitness. Only when you are healthy and feel good about yourself, can you take care of your partner. So, remember to eat right, stay fit, and sleep well. A healthy body results in a healthy mind and that clearly reflects in your relationship. Remain attractive to both of you. This increases the sexiness of all the other activities.

### Spend Time Together

While adding on cuckolding, it is important to spend quality time together with just the two of you. Going out with the kids is not considered quality time together. You still need date night and maybe picnics in the park, bike rides or just hanging out. I can recall a couple who was married for 27 years and introduced all sorts of extras into the relationship, and they had lunch together every single day to simply talk. It worked. Their relationship was able to withstand any obstacle.

## Give Her Space

Being in a relationship doesn't mean that you have to be together every second of the day. She still needs to meet with her friends and you still need the beer night with the boys. Allow each other to have time to spend alone as well.

## Help with Chores

There is a reason why 80 percent of women complain about being too tired to have sex or do anything. Women have to excel in their careers and take care of the kids, the household and your needs. It's an exhausting life. Any help you give to your Queen will help her and keep her in a sexier mood.

## Make Her Feel Special

Every day is an opportunity to make your Queen feel special. You have so many chances to compliment her, leave her love notes, bring her flowers and make her feel like she is the luckiest person in the world. Not only will she be in a better mood, she will respond in a positive way and it keeps the focus on you and not the cuckolding as much. The truth is, every interaction we have with another person, even someone we've known for a long time, is a new possibility for lively connection. It often takes only a small action—a sweet smile, a flirtatious look, or an act of affection to turn a mundane interaction into an exciting one. These are simple ways to make your Queen feel special. Check her out, give her that sexy look like she is the most gorgeous woman on the planet.

## Keep Touching

Touch is so important in relationships. Whether it's kissing, handholding, hugging, or cuddling—all keep the spice alive. Touch her hair, her back and her legs often. Squeeze her butt as you go by. Give her a kiss for no reason and hold hands. Touch keeps the focus on you both.

## Set the Scene

Just as you would prepare for your big night of cuckolding, you also need to keep the primary space sexy. Draw her a bath, lay out some lingerie, get her favorite bubbles, get some wine or champagne and massage oils. You want to show dedication and effort. Men always complain that they don't understand why women are upset. Women want the fantasy without having to explain each and every step. You want to show this woman that even though you engage in open relationships the primary relationship is what you need. Make a special dinner with candlelight for her. There is no need to wait for a special moment to make her feel special and loved.

## Have Sex Regularly

Your sex life still needs to be great and regular. Cuckolding is not going to fix a boring sex life or any other issues in the relationship. So, it is going to be very important that you have a great sex life and you keep it alive. You can reserve certain acts for cuckolding while engaging in others in your intimate times. For example, you can reserve oral and anal sex for your own sex times. It is recommended that your own sex be where you connect deeply as a couple.

## Be Truthful

Studies have found that people who are truthful about themselves experience more relationship intimacy and well-being, and better romantic relationships. Overall, studies find that positive connection and intimacy grow when you are transparent about what's inside of you. A recent study by the University of Georgia looked at the connection between communication and the degree of satisfaction reported by couples. It found that good communication in itself could not account for how satisfied partners were with a relationship over time.

The researchers recognize that other factors must influence couples' satisfaction, and that good communication can result from those factors. According to Justin Lavner, lead author of the study, found that more satisfied couples communicate better on average than those who are less satisfied. So, what is going to make you and your Queen more satisfied is the happiness you feel together and being truthful and honest about your feelings throughout your exploration.

# CHAPTER **18**

# Woman's Needs in an Open Relationship

W omen will always be the one to be criticized in an open relationship, so their needs must be honored. Men have always had the freedom to do what they want—cheat, have threesomes, crave cuckolding, and do group sex—but if a woman admits to doing any of those, she is labeled "a whore," "unstable," or "sex maniac." Today, times are changing. Women are demanding to have the same rights to do what they want with their lives and relationships. They require you to be open and supportive in the adventure, if it's to go well.

Here are some of the rights women need. They have the right, without shame, blame or guilt in all intimate relationships, to be free from male coercion, male violence and male intimidation. They should be able to choose how they want to conduct themselves in open relationships. Women have the need to explore their emotions and to communicate all of their feminine needs as they set the rules and boundaries that are to be respected by you if you have consented to an open relationship.

They need to know that you are on board to satisfy their needs in sex and cuckolding, and you will be supportive no matter what happens. Why is this important? Because men will criticize women having this much control. In a Female Led Relationship, it is the woman who decides how many partners she wants, the level of time and investment and what sexual pleasures she will offer to each male partner. Although she is leading, she will do so in a loving and compassionate way and will discuss openly with you and anyone else involved.

Your role as the primary male is to "wait at home," pursue a "non-sexual experience" or spend time with friends, while she goes out. You will learn to do your best to overcome your desire to control the situation during her outings. You must accept your role and duty as her supporter. If you feel fearful, jealous, panicked or some other unpleasant emotion, you must communicate this to your Queen, so you can work it out.

It is at the sole discretion of the Queen as female leader, whether you will also be allowed to have relationships with outside connections. As the male primary partner, you will always respect her command and follow her direction in all cases. For example, if you are both on vacation and she decides she wants to explore with another person, then you can discuss how it will unfold but she will ultimately lead in how it unfolds. She makes the first move and directs you.

The Queen will be free to make commitments and accept responsibility for her actions. Her freedom comes from the personal expression of her own power. No one can take away the female's power to be herself and to lead the relationship. The *Love & Obey* female chooses freely to help empower her partner, not to humiliate him or abuse him. She chooses to love, honor, and respect in exchange for your 100 percent absolute obedience to her will.

As you have read, this book is for couples who are deeply committed and choose to embark on shared sexually open experiences with outside individuals. These open experiences will definitely set aside the traditional rules of a monogamous relationship or marriage. I have shown you that you need to promise to each other to be open, honest and loyal at all times during this experience. Under no circumstances will you lie or mislead one another. Your Queen will need to trust you and herself.

# CHAPTER 19

# Alternative Forms of Cuckolding

C uckolding occurs alone without the man's participation. The main suggestion in this book was that both men and women should partake in cuckolding together. This ensures that the relationship stays sound and both people feel involved. But sometimes the Queen decides that she wants to see the Bull alone. Should this occur, know what the safeguards are. In the show *Succession*, Shiv Roy decides that she wants to see men outside of the relationship and she does this without the presence of her husband. While this can leave you feeling ignored and left out, it can be an important evolution to allow her to do it.

First, it establishes trust. If you cannot trust her to carry this out and return to you, then there is an issue in the relationship. By allowing her to have the freedom, you are giving her complete loyalty and devotion. However, this kind of freedom must be done responsibly. It will be important to review the rules and, of course, have a discussion after. Many couples may have an intimate moment after the Queen returns home to maintain a bond. In this scenario, it may be important to agree that only certain acts will be allowed and others forbidden. If she sticks to the rules, then allowing her the freedom to do it alone may not be such a bad thing.

## Cuckolding with a Woman

Most cuckolding acts involve another man, the Bull who is generally more well-endowed. But sometimes the cuckolding is done with a woman. Some men think this is the best of both worlds because they assume it will be a threesome. But generally, cuckolding with a woman will not be done together with you, so it could have some challenges. One of the main rules is the outside partner or Bull should never be someone you could develop an emotional relationship with. Does this include your Queen developing a relationship with a woman? It will be important to review the rules and ensure the strength of the primary relationship. If cuckolding is to happen with a woman, there should be clear boundaries established and no development of an emotional bond. This also applies to you attempting to meet the outside woman as well. There are all sorts of ways this could go wrong.

## Cuckolding Followed by the Man Cleaning the Queen

In some cuckolding relationships, there is a desire to be the sissy cuck who shows his devotion by performing oral sex on the Queen after she has been with the Bull. Whereas, this is a show of complete submission, and it must only be done with your full consent and not as part of a scheme to punish you in a BDSM scenario. *Love & Obey* is a loving Female Led Relationship and the same is true of cuckolding. It should never be done as part of a way to punish the man. So, while couples engage in this scenario, it is best to establish what the rules are and what will be allowed. Don't be afraid to speak up about your fantasies. If it is your desire to serve your Queen this way, then you may proceed. It is important to establish the rules to ensure everyone is on board.

### The Sissy Cuck

In cuckolding, you will often find men who want to be feminine while being in the cuck role. They want to wear women's underwear and lingerie, and they want to sit in silence while the more dominant Queen expresses her control by being with her Bull in front of him or she chooses to go outside and meet the Bull privately, telling the cuck about her adventure. Many Female Led Relationships began like this and the men even provided "homosexual" services to the Bulls as well. The women made the men suck the Bull and get him ready to penetrate her. Cuckolding presents the opportunity for the woman to decide how she wants to run this experience and that is the difference with female led cuckolding. Men also decide how feminine and submissive they choose to be in the experience.

## Engage in Cuckolding as Punishment

Many times, in relationships, we can get very angry and say things we do not mean. In cuckolding, it would be very easy to use it as a threat to a man. Your Queen may say, "I'm going to sleep with another man because I am angry with you." While arguments do happen and people can exchange angry words, cuckolding should never be used to punish. First of all, doing so violates the important trust in the relationship where men and women must give their consent. If it is used as punishment, you can be left with a very negative feeling about it which can lead to harboring ill-feelings. Where cuckolding should be adding excitement and adventure to the relationship, it should not add fear and dishonesty. This takes things too far into the cheating realm. Left unchecked this could turn out into a way, you hurt each other and the relationship.

## Engaging in Cuckolding with Another Couple

This may seem like it's the same as wife swapping but it's not. Cuckolding with another couple could consist of you watching while she is with two other men, she is with a man and a woman, or she is with two other women. All of these are options, but they do come with their own challenges. Now it's more important to ensure there are no feelings of jealousy or being left out. You should fully discuss with her how it will unfold and what will be each of your roles. You will have to be particularly OK with how the man and woman engage with your Queen and stick to the rules and boundaries. Perhaps there is no oral sex received or given. Maybe there will only be one act being performed at one time or everyone is participating. These alternatives should only be done once you are successful with the simple version. The more partners, the more you would have to deal with.

# CHAPTER **20**

# The Keys to Cuckolding in a Female Led a Relationship

In a Female Led Relationship, the rules for cuckolding are skewed to give the female complete control but there are still some things that can be done to ensure a smooth experience. The following are the keys to cuckolding in an FLR.

## Key # 1. Both partners must deal with feelings of jealousy.

It is natural to feel possessive and jealous in the few times of embarking in cuckolding. The way for you to deal with jealousy is to understand why you are engaging in cuckolding and ensuring that you and you Queen are on the same page.

You may have the inclination to say:

- "I'm jealous. I don't look like those hot guys you were checking out."

- "I got really jealous when you went down on my girlfriend like that."

- "I'm feeling a little jealous and trying to get through it."

- "I know you love me, but I need some reassurances."

The minute you say, "I'm jealous" out loud, it stops being as negative and destructive a force and becomes a signal to your partner that you need some attention and reinforcement. The key to getting past these feelings is to address it in an open fashion. You and your Queen need to be understanding and patient through the process, and be willing to abort if it seems too overwhelming. Hence, the need to do everything together.

The key to being in a Female Led Relationship is that while this may be something initiated for your Queen's pleasure, you need to be 100 percent in agreement. There is no point to lying or trying to hide your feelings as these will lead to resentment and destruction of your relationship. If you are having these feelings, you must refrain from outbursts and displays of anger. Know that this is something that can be resolved in a peaceful manner.

Whatever you and Queen decide to do, whether insisting on monogamy or making certain exceptions, that is for them alone to decide. What matters is that once you've decided and agreed upon the terms of your relationship, you must stand by these decisions. In doing so, you offer trust, freedom and respect as the separate individuals they are. When two people recognize each other's individuality, they're able to avoid falling into a fake bond, which is an illusion of connection that replaces real love and sabotages exciting relationships. They're able to maintain their attractions to each other and to keep the spark alive, so to speak.

To avoid a fake bond and other traps that doom any relationship, all couples should strive to be honest with each other, to deal with their jealous feelings in healthy ways and to challenge their deeply rooted fears of intimacy. By making this their focus, they are far better able to sustain richer, more rewarding relationships. They are much better equipped to have open, honest and mature discussions about attractions and monogamy and are much less likely to engage in deception and secret infidelity.

## Key # 2. *You Both Reinforce Your Love*

There is a reason you and your Queen are in a relationship. There is love. It takes real love to want to see your partner be very happy and do what is necessary to ensure you serve your Queen. So, the key to successful cuckolding is to remember and reinforce the love as the primary partners in your relationship. No one can destroy a bond, which is strong and made of real love. Your desire to explore does not diminish your love for each other. So, celebrate it.

Cuckolding can make you feel like you are not enough to satisfy her; it can spark a huge ego flare-up in some men. They take it as they are not worthy, good enough or manly enough to satisfy the Queen. But the truth is, women can love you and just need some outside experience. How many men has said cheating did not really matter—it was just sex. The same is for your Queen who may have the desire for cuckolding. It doesn't mean she loves you less or more. She loves you. She doesn't want you to change "or fix" anything about you. She wants you fully in her life and not on the sidelines. She wants you right there, in the inner fold of her female passion and her loving authority. You need to know that when she has a sexual attraction to someone else or a romantic connection with someone else, it doesn't invalidate your love, and it doesn't lessen what she feels for you. In fact, it can make her love you more because you understand she has needs.

## Key # 3. Your Queen Makes the Rules

She leads your relationship and you must obey her, but you may feel the need to confront her about a major issue like taking on a new lover. However, you should be a team player with her. Do not be disobedient or back her into a corner— that will be a mistake.

- "We're not getting out of this car until we talk."

- "You're not leaving this house until we talk."

Don't say things like that to her. That is disobedient and backing her into a corner. You don't corner your Mistress and demand conversation. You don't make ultimatums. You don't withhold your services, sexual or otherwise because she is not doing what you want. She is in charge and has every right to do what she wants; you made the choice to be in a Female Led Relationship, and it is not for you to decide.

Look at it like you're both "partners-in-love" or co-workers hatching a new project. Your teammates with a new "big game" coming up. Look at it like you're doing this together. Sometimes you will have to pick up the slack. Sometimes they'll have to pick up the slack. When there's a problem, cornering a teammate, a co-worker or a life-partner and making demands is not the best way to work things out. Instead, talk things out and plan out this new adventure together.

## Key # 4. Do Everything Together

I have stressed this for a reason. The couples who play together, stay together. These adventures are just that—exploration, and they must be done together with the consent of all parties involved. You and your Queen make the decisions together of how to engage in many of the forms of open relationships so you can respect your relationship. Your main relationship takes priority, and all other adventures, including cuckolding, should be done together.

## Key # 5. Be Loving and Kind

Scientists have made efforts to classify different types of love. Recently, researcher Dr. Barbara Acevedo discovered some good news about one type in particular. "Romantic love," the kind that is characterized by "intensity, engagement and sexual interest" can last a lifetime. Neuroscientists have even discovered that the brains of couples who experience this kind of love can keep firing for each other the same way they did when they first met even 20 or so years later. Romantic love is associated with marital satisfaction, well-being, high self-esteem and relationship longevity. You want to invest in building romantic love by being loving.

In Female Led Relationships, we are dealing with strong dominant women, who do what they want and the men who submit to their desires. Still for many couples, the man's ego and pride are still a factor and sometimes he doesn't want to know, even though he knows. So, we can be driven to be mean and critical out of emotions we may feel while engaging in cuckolding. However, I think open and honest communication is a key to a long-term successful, open relationship. I think couples should show a loving kindness.

When we meet someone new, it is easy to feel what scientists Elaine Hatfield and Richard Rapson describe as passionate love, which they state is "a state of intense longing for union with another." But there can be an obsessive element, characterized by intrusive thinking, uncertainty, and mood swings. So, this type of love can work well in the beginning of relationships, but can be hurtful in the long run. During cuckolding, it is easy to feel swept away with the newness of it all, but it will be extremely important to focus on the real love—the romantic love you have between you and the Queen.

Kindness was found to be the most important characteristic in a relationship. It beat out physical attractiveness, good financial prospects, humor, chastity, religiosity, the desire for children, and creativity. Kindness is defined as the quality of being friendly, generous, and considerate. When we have negative views of ourselves, it's difficult to be kind toward others. If we lack self-compassion and have harsh, judgmental attitudes toward ourselves, we extend those same feelings toward others. Therefore, it is necessary to start with being kind to yourself. Once you are happy with yourself, this will transfer to your partner. Kindness to your Queen and vice versa is one of the greatest gifts you can give each other.

# Conclusion

Cuckolding is becoming one of the most fascinating sexual activities in relationships, and there is growing interest in it from both men and women. A cuckold is someone who takes pleasure in watching their partner have sex with someone else. Today, cuckolding is more than just sex. There can be complex issues at play and quite often men and women are both interested in exploring it. As a couple, it is important that you both explore together and maintain open channels of communication with each other and the Bull. There are so many exciting ways to explore but focus must remain on the primary relationship. Open relationships are becoming more popular, but regardless of what you engage in, you and the Queen must be on the same page. This can be accomplished with an agreement, which helps to lay down all rules. Cuckolding, unlike history has described it, has been found to be a positive activity in relationships. Critics have tried to describe it in a negative way, but with consent from all parties, cuckolding can be the very experience that spices up your primary relationship. Avoid the pitfalls and be open with your woman, and it can be a very fulfilling experience.

Made in the USA
Las Vegas, NV
24 September 2023

78095393R00079